The Most Desperate Acts of Gallantry

GEORGE A. CUSTER IN THE CIVIL WAR

by Daniel T. Davis

EMERGING CIVIL WAR SERIES

Chris Mackowski, series editor
Chris Kolakowski, chief historian

The Emerging Civil War Series

offers compelling, easy-to-read overviews of some of the Civil War's most important battles and stories.

Recipient of the Army Historical Foundation's Lieutenant General Richard G. Trefry Award for contributions to the literature on the history of the U.S. Army

Other titles in the Emerging Civil War Series by Daniel T. Davis:

Bloody Autumn: The Shenandoah Valley Campaign of 1864
by Daniel T. Davis and Phillip S. Greenwalt

Calamity in Carolina: The Battles of Averasboro and Bentonville, March 1865
by Daniel T. Davis and Phillip S. Greenwalt

Don't Give an Inch: The Second Day at Gettysburg–From Little Round Top to Cemetery Ridge, July 2, 1863
by Chris Mackowski, Kristopher D. White, and Daniel T. Davis

Fight Like the Devil: The First Day at Gettysburg, July 1, 1863
by Chris Mackowski, Kristopher D. White, and Daniel T. Davis

Hurricane from the Heavens: The Battle of Cold Harbor, May 26-June 5, 1864
by Daniel T. Davis and Phillip S. Greenwalt

Out Flew the Sabres: The Battle of Brandy Station, June 9, 1863
by Eric J. Wittenberg and Daniel T. Davis

Other titles in the Emerging Civil War Series:

The Last Road North: A Guide to the Gettysburg Campaign, 1863
by Robert Orrison and Dan Welch

That Field of Blood: The Battle of Antietam, September 17, 1862
by Daniel Vermilya

For a complete list of titles in the Emerging Civil War Series, visit www.emergingcivilwar.com.

The Most Desperate Acts of Gallantry

GEORGE A. CUSTER IN THE CIVIL WAR

by Daniel T. Davis

EMERGING CIVIL WAR SERIES

SB

Savas Beatie

California

First edition, first printing

ISBN-13 (paperback): 978-1-61121-411-6
ISBN-13 (ebook): 978-1-61121-412-3

Library of Congress Cataloging-in-Publication Data

Names: Davis, Daniel T., 1982- author.
Title: The most desperate acts of gallantry : George A. Custer in the Civil War / by Daniel T. Davis.
Other titles: George A. Custer in the Civil War
Description: First edition. | El Dorado Hills, California : Savas Beatie, [2018]
Identifiers: LCCN 2018018061| ISBN 9781611214116 (pbk : alk. paper) | ISBN 9781611214123 (ebk)
Subjects: LCSH: Custer, George A. (George Armstrong), 1839-1876. | United States. Army. Michigan Cavalry Brigade (1862-1865)--Biography. | United States--History--Civil War, 1861-1865--Cavalry operations. | United States. Army--Officers--Biography. | United States--History--Civil War, 1861-1865--Campaigns.
Classification: LCC E514.6 .D38 2018 | DDC 973.8/2092 [B] --dc23
LC record available at https://lccn.loc.gov/2018018061

SB

Published by
Savas Beatie LLC
989 Governor Drive, Suite 102
El Dorado Hills, California 95762
Phone: 916-941-6896
Email: sales@savasbeatie.com
Web: www.savasbeatie.com

Savas Beatie titles are available at special discounts for bulk purchases in the United States by corporations, institutions, and other organizations. For more details, please contact Special Sales, 989 Governor Drive, Suite 102, El Dorado Hills, CA 95762, or you may e-mail us at sales@savasbeatie.com, or visit our website at www.savasbeatie.com for additional information.

For Katy
my wife, my love, my best friend

Table of Contents

Footnotes for this volume are available at
http://emergingcivilwar.com/publications/the-emerging-civil-war-series/footnotes

A Civil War Trails marker alongside Route 15 north of Frederick, Maryland, tells the story of Custer's sudden promotion to brigadier general during the Gettysburg campaign. (cm)

List of Maps

Maps by Hal Jespersen

Acknowledgments

In July 1881, Lt. Charles Roe and a company from the 2nd U.S. Cavalry erected this obelisk on Last Stand Hill. The grassy area surrounding the monument is a mass grave that contains the remains of soldiers from the 7th Cavalry who died in the battle. Custer's body was found in the right foreground. (dd)

I have been fascinated by the story of George Armstrong Custer for as long as I can remember. There are a number of people that deserve my heartfelt thanks in seeing this effort to completion. Chris Mackowksi and Kris White founded Emerging Civil War in 2011 and gave me an opportunity to write about something I love. Chris also proofed, edited, and made key suggestions to the manuscript that made it better. To them I say, "Thank you."

Ted Savas, Sarah Keeney, and the wonderful folks at Savas Beatie, LLC, continue to provide tremendous support throughout many of my publication ventures.

Historians Chris Kolakowski and Edward Alexander reviewed and provided suggestions on the original manuscript, as did my old pard, great friend, and frequent collaborator, Phill Greenwalt.

Eric J. Wittenberg, another frequent collaborator and the authority of Civil War cavalry operations, also read the manuscript, gave me excellent advice, and contributed a wonderful foreword. My dear friend Ashley Webb wrote an excellent appendix on Custer's marriage. (As always, my best to you and Mike.) Respected author and historian Paul Ashdown also penned a fantastic appendix. Cartographer Hal Jespersen put together a great set of maps.

Bert Dunkerly offered insight on New Bridge. So, too, did Rob Orrison on Buckland Mills, Alyssa Bingham on Appomattox Station, and Zachary

Pittard on Sailor's Creek. Kevin and Kristen Pawlak gave time out of their day to go over the Kearneysville battlefield, a place where Custer extricated his command in the face of a superior foe. I thoroughly enjoyed my conversations with the exceptional historians at the Little Bighorn Battlefield National Monument, Mike Donahue and Steve Adelson, which gave me further insight and consideration into Custer's last battle.

To my wonderful parents, Tommy and Kathy Davis, and my in-laws Cathy and the late Thomas Bowen: thank you for everything you have done and continue to do for me. Tom: we miss you and we love you. Thanks also go out to my brother, Matt, his wife, Candice, and our nephew Brett, and my sister and brother-in-law, Becca and Andy, and our dear nieces, Elinor and Amelia. My wife's cousin and great buddy Rick Bowen is always a joy to talk to and is a patient sounding board for anything related to Custer. As always, I look forward to my weekly discussions with my great uncle Bill Green, Sr. I also owe a special thanks to my uncle Frank Allen, who took time out of a vacation to get pictures that are included in one of the appendices. To all of my family, friends, and colleagues: thank you all.

And to my wonderful wife, Katy, for her unending love, patience and support.

PHOTO CREDITS: Frank Allen (fa); *Battles & Leaders of the Civil War* (b&l); Dan Davis (dd); *Generals in Gray* (gig); Katy Bowen-Davis (kb-d); Library of Congress (loc); Chris Mackowski (cm); National Archives (na); National Park Service, Little Bighorn Battlefield National Monument (nps, lbhbnm)

For the Emerging Civil War Series

Theodore P. Savas, *publisher*
Chris Mackowski, *series editor*
Chris Kolakowski, *chief historian*
Sarah Keeney, *editorial consultant*
Kristopher D. White, *co-founding editor*

Maps by Hal Jespersen
Design and layout by Tara Hatmaker

$\mathscr{F}$oreword

BY ERIC J. WITTENBERG

Few figures have left more of an indelible imprint on the history of the last 150 years than has George Armstrong Custer. Rising to very high rank at a precocious age, Custer leapt into the public consciousness when, at the tender age of 23, he was promoted from brevet captain to brigadier general of volunteers. Custer, who finished dead last in his class at West Point, had never commanded anything larger than a single scouting expedition before the spring of 1863, when he was suddenly and unexpectedly catapulted into brigade command just a few days before the battle of Gettysburg.

Custer's utter lack of experience in command meant that he had never learned Army politics and certainly had never learned regimental politics. There was a good reason for this lapse—except for brief stretches, he served almost exclusively as a staff officer before his promotion. But Army of the Potomac Cavalry Corps commander Alfred Pleasonton—Custer's patron and mentor—appreciated Custer's aggressiveness and zeal, so Pleasonton made sure that the young man was promoted over much more senior officers to take command of a brigade of four regiments of Michigan cavalry.

Custer made an immediate impression, wearing an outrageous and distinctive uniform that made him look like "a circus rider gone mad," as one observer noted. He made his mark on his first day commanding troops in the field at the June 30, 1863,

Efforts to erect a monument to Custer in his adopted state of Michigan began in 1906. A group of citizens from Monroe and the Michigan Cavalry Brigade Association petitioned the legislature, and a year later, the governor signed a bill that appropriated $25,000 for the statue. Monroe was chosen as the location for the monument, which—at the suggestion of Libbie Custer—would depict the moment Custer first spotted Maj. Gen. James Ewell Brown "Jeb" Stuart's mounted force on East Cavalry Field at Gettysburg on July 3, 1863. Known as *Sighting the Enemy*, the monument was dedicated on June 4, 1910. Mrs. Custer, President William Taft, and 25,000 citizens attended the ceremony. The statue was moved from Loranger Square to its present location in 1923. (fa)

The frieze on the Michigan Cavalry Brigade monument at Gettysburg depicts the charge of the 1st Michigan Cavalry at climax of the fight on East Cavalry Field. (dd)

battle of Hanover, Pennsylvania. Custer led his brigade there with credit. His good luck nearly ran out two days later at the battle of Hunterstown, when he led an audacious charge, had his horse shot out from under him and pin him by its fall. Fortunately, his orderly, Norvill Churchill, came along and rescued him, setting the stage for the drama that played out the next day.

Major General J. E. B. Stuart's vaunted Confederate cavalry operated on the far left flank of the Army of Northern Virginia on July 3, 1863. Stuart's primary task was to guard Lee's flank, but he also had the discretion to try to sortie behind the Federal center if the opportunity presented itself. When Stuart attempted to do so, Custer, blonde locks blowing in the wind, cried out, "Come on you Wolverines!" and led a saber charge that abruptly ended Stuart's lone attempt to get into the Federal rear.

The Gettysburg campaign served as a launching pad for Custer's career, and by the late summer of 1864, he had been promoted to divisional command. Custer led the 3rd Cavalry Division for the rest of the Civil War, routing his old West Point friend and classmate's cavalry at the battle of Tom's Brook on October 9, 1864. His troopers, who, by then, idolized him, proudly wore their red "Custer Neckties" to show that they served under his command.

The 3rd Division's attack on the Confederate right flank at Five Forks helped to shatter the gray line there, and then Custer's troopers got across the Army of Northern Virginia's line of retreat at Appomattox Station, where they captured the supplies so desperately needed by Robert E. Lee's gray tatterdemalions. Deprived of supplies, and with their route of retreat cut off, Lee found himself with no alternative but surrender on April 9, 1865. A jubilant Maj. Gen. Philip H. Sheridan, the cavalry corps commander, purchased the table that the surrender instrument had been written on and made a gift of it to Custer as a token of his esteem and of his gratitude for all that Custer had done to bring the Civil War to a close.

Sadly for Custer, his naiveté of army politics, his inexperience with regimental command, and his poor decisions—such as attacking President Ulysses S. Grant's younger brother, Orvil, and Secretary of War William Belknap—brought him within a whisker

of losing his military career. Nevertheless, Custer earned the reputation of being a fierce and successful Indian fighter—a reputation that was suddenly lost on the banks of the Little Bighorn River in Montana on June 25, 1876. That day, Custer's now legendary good luck ran out, and he, along with his brothers Tom and Boston, his nephew Autie Reed, and 265 of the troopers of his 7th Cavalry died at the hands of Sioux and Northern Cheyenne Indians.

It's easy to view Custer solely in the light of how he died. I admit that there was a time when I did. In spite of the debacle that hot, dusty June day in 1876, Custer's remarkable record of success during the Civil War is almost unparalleled. *The Most Desperate Acts of Gallantry,* Daniel T. Davis's latest entry into the Emerging Civil War book series, does a fine job of telling that story. Davis highlights Custer's many brave deeds and battlefield successes in a clear and concise fashion.

Ride with Custer and his legendary Wolverines as they make their mark on Civil War battlefield after Civil War battlefield.

A squadron of the 6th Michigan Calvary under Maj. Peter Weber charges Brig. Gen. J.J. Pettigrew's North Carolinians at Falling Waters during the Gettyburg Campaign. (loc)

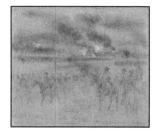

Custer's 3rd Cavalry Division marched down the Shenandoah Valley in October 1864. (loc)

ERIC J. WITTENBERG *is the award-winning author of more than twenty books and an acknowledged expert on Federal cavalry during the Civil War.*

"Mistakes have not been an uncommon thing
with men of greatness in all pursuits of life.
It is the natural thing. The outcome of a military
campaign cannot be predetermined by the
precision of mathematics or philosophy.
Custer—he was the 'go get 'em' type of soldier."
— Walter Camp

Prologue

A small party of men crested the ridge ahead of the troopers. With the battalion following closely behind, they went on at a gallop. Dirt thrown up by the horses mingled in the air and settled into a thick, choking cloud. There was little wind to alleviate the heat. As the men slowed to a trot, they grabbed for canteens and wiped sweat from their brows. Just several yards ahead of them, their regimental commander reigned in his horse at the edge of the bluff.

His appearance did not meet army regulations, but on campaign, it was much more comfortable than the standard officer's uniform. The shirt was double breasted with military buttons. His trousers were made of buckskin and were tucked into his boots. A broad hat with the right brim turned up helped to ward off the Northern Plains sun. He had already fastened his fringed buckskin shirt to the back of his saddle in an effort to stay cool.

As he rode along, Lt. Col. George Armstrong Custer carefully studied and analyzed the scene below him. Rather than swarming like a hive of hornets, very little action showed among the tepees. Exuberant, he removed his hat, turned to his men, and shouted, "Courage boys, we will get them, and as soon as we get through we will go back to our station."

Four days earlier, Custer and his regiment had been encamped at the mouth of Rosebud Creek near the Yellowstone River in eastern Montana Territory. That afternoon, Custer met with Col. John Gibbon and Brig. Gen. Alfred Terry aboard the steamer *Far West*. His regiment, the 7th United States Cavalry, had

The 7th U.S. Cavalry camped near the Yellowstone River on June 21, 1876. "We . . . are fitting up for a scout under Genl. Custer with 12 companies of cavalry up the [R]osebud across to the Bighorn River & down that," wrote Acting Assistant Surgeon James DeWolf. Sadly, DeWolf lost his life in the coming battle. (dd)

George Armstrong Custer in campaign attire. His buckskin jackets are on display at the Little Bighorn Battlefield National Monument and at the Smithsonian. (nps, lbhbnm)

Sitting Bull, the powerful Hunkpapa medicine man. (loc)

been in the field for a little over a month in an effort to locate and return hostile members of the Sioux and Northern Cheyenne tribes under the great medicine man Sitting Bull to their reservation. A battalion from his regiment under Maj. Marcus A. Reno had recently returned from a reconnaissance across the Tongue River and Rosebud Creek, tributaries of the Yellowstone. Reno had found a fresh trail along the Rosebud. Based on this information, Terry decided to send Custer with his entire regiment to follow the trail. Gibbon's column, made up mostly of infantry, was to march along the Yellowstone to the mouth of the Bighorn River and situate itself opposite Custer. Terry hoped to trap Sitting Bull's village in a pincer.

Terry provided orders for Custer to follow during his march but gave him the discretion to act as the situation warranted. Custer, in turn, passed on supply instructions to the regimental officers. "We were to transport on our pack-mules fifteen days' rations of hard bread, coffee, and sugar; twelve days' rations," wrote 1st Lt. Edward Godfrey, in command of Company K. "Each man was to be supplied with 100 rounds of carbine ammunition and 24 rounds of pistol ammunition, to be carried on his person and in his saddle-bags."

Late that night, Custer stole a few moments to write a hasty letter to his wife, Libbie. "I have but a few moments to write as we start at twelve," he wrote. "I have my hands full of preparations for the scout. Do not be anxious for me. . . . I hope to have a good report to send you by the next mail."

By noon on June 22, 1876, the 7th Cavalry was prepared to march. Gibbon and Terry rode to the end of the camp to watch as Custer and his regiment departed. "Together we sat on our horses and witnessed the approach of the command as it threaded its way through the rank sage brush which covered the valley," Gibbon wrote. "The regiment presented a fine appearance. . . . Custer appeared to be in good spirits, chatted freely with us, and was evidently proud of the appearance of his command."

With the approach of the rear guard, Custer turned to Gibbon and Terry and shook hands with them. "As he turned to leave us I made some pleasant remark, warning against being greedy," Gibbon remembered. Custer waved his hand and called back, "No, I will not," as he rode away.

Custer assumed a leisurely pace and covered about a dozen miles in four hours before calling a halt. After supper, he passed the word for an officers' call, and the men gathered. He began the conference by ordering that all bugle calls be suspended unless in an emergency. The bugles might otherwise give them away. In that event, it was quite likely the village would break up and the various bands would scatter—a situation Custer could ill-afford.

Each day's march began at 5 a.m., and Custer went on giving out the responsibilities of "reveille, stables, watering, halting and grazing" to the company commanders. Only orders for when to move out in the morning and when to bivouac would come from Custer. "He took particular pains to impress upon the officers his reliance upon their judgement, discretion and loyalty," 1st Lieutenant Godfrey recalled. Based on the information gathered by Reno's scout, Custer told those assembled that he expected to encounter around one thousand warriors but probably no more than fifteen hundred.

The conversation, to some, was "extraordinary for General Custer for it was not his habit to unbosom

"Little did we think we had seen him for the last time, or imagine under what circumstances we should next see that command, now mounting the bluffs in the distance with its little guidons gayly fluttering in the breeze," John Gibbon recalled as he watched Custer and his regiment ride away from the Yellowstone. (loc)

After departing Terry's command, the 7th Cavalry followed Rosebud Creek in search of Sitting Bull's village. (dd)

A marker stands in the Rosebud Valley where the 7th Cavalry spent the night of June 22, 1876. (dd)

himself to his officers," Godfrey wrote. "In it he showed a lack of self-confidence, a reliance on somebody else; there was an indefinable something that was not Custer." Before the group was dismissed, all present synchronized their watches. In the darkness, the officers walked back to their companies. Godfrey ambled along accompanied by 1st Lts. Donald McIntosh and George Wallace. Then Wallace broke the silence. "Godfrey, I believe General Custer is going to be killed."

"Why, Wallace?" Godfrey responded. "What makes you think so?"

"Because I have never heard Custer talk in that way before."

As prescribed, at five the next morning, the regiment resumed its journey along the Rosebud. Eight miles into the ride, it encountered the remains of a large village. "Every bend of the stream bore traces of some old camp, and their ponies had nipped almost every spear of grass," Wallace wrote. "The ground was strewn with broken bones and cuttings from buffalo hides." Continuing on, the soldiers found three more campsites. Custer called a halt at each one to allow the Crow and Ree scouts to study the tracks. Around 5 p.m., Custer stopped for the day after covering around thirty-three miles.

Evidence of a large Indian encampment grew as Custer and the regiment continued their ride on June 24. He slowed to allow the scouts to investigate and inspect the camp sites. "The valley was heavily marked with lodge-pole trails and pony tracks, showing that an immense herd of ponies had been driven over it," Godfrey wrote. Custer also inspected the remains. Signs were fresh, and as the day wore on, he surmised the village could not be more than a day-and-a-half journey ahead. This proximity caused him to take additional precautions. Custer ordered his men to ride on either side of the creek so as not to form a large dust cloud and give away their presence. Shortly after sundown, the regiment made camp.

Around dark, Custer went to visit his scouts. The trail they had been following clearly turned toward the Little Bighorn River. The Crows, long-time enemies of the Sioux, informed him about a high point atop a hill that divided the Rosebud and Little Bighorn valleys. From there, they might be able to locate the village. Custer ordered 2nd Lt. Charles Varnum, who was in charge of the scouts, to ride ahead and reach the spot, known as the Crow's Nest, before daylight. After Varnum set out, Custer returned to his bivouac and summoned his officers. He informed them the regiment would march immediately to reach the

This small monument marks the area of the Seventh's camp on June 23. A plaque, which has since been removed, read, "Custer camped here June 23, 1876." (dd)

On the third day of the march, Custer passed through Sitting Bull's Sun Dance camp, part of which can be seen in the photo. This annual religious ceremony was sacred to the Sioux and had occurred just weeks before. While participating in the dance, Sitting Bull had a vision of soldiers falling upside down into the Sioux camp. It served as great inspiration to the warriors and was an omen of things to come. (dd)

The Wolf Mountains, seen in the distance, divided the Rosebud and Little Bighorn valleys. (dd)

divide before dawn. Custer planned to use June 25 to reconnoiter the approaches to the village and then attack the following day.

With darkness covering the landscape, the 7th trotted on. "The night was very calm, but occasionally a slight breeze would waft . . . and disconcert our bearings," Godfrey remembered. "We were obliged to halt to catch a sound from those in advance, sometimes whistling or hallooing, and getting a response we would start forward again."

About 2 a.m., Custer reined in his command. Some of the troopers took advantage of the moment and unsaddled their horses. Others brewed coffee as the summer sun peeked over the eastern horizon.

Custer found a small patch of sage brush and laid down to rest—but it was not long before he was awakened from his nap with a message from Varnum. The scouts had indeed spotted a village in the Little Bighorn valley. Custer passed the word to his officers for the regiment to mount up and follow on to the divide.

On his approach, Custer discerned a rider coming toward him. It was Varnum himself. The lieutenant reaffirmed his initial report, but he also had more news to share. After he had dispatched the message, his party had spotted two braves who had approached and then moved through the divide. They must have seen the regiment, as they quickly split up and rode off in different directions. About the same time, Varnum had caught sight of a larger party of about a dozen Sioux. They too dispersed as the regiment approached. Varnum then escorted

Custer to Crow's Nest. Unlike his Crow scouts, Custer struggled to locate the village. After several minutes, he finally gave up and said, "Well, I've got about as good as eyes as anybody and I can't see any village, Indians or otherwise."

Shortly after, Custer left the divide and returned to the regiment. When he reached the column, his brother, Capt. Thomas W. Custer, greeted him with alarming news. Some troopers had returned to the back trail to retrieve a box of hardtack lost in the night, and on their way, they encountered several Sioux, who quickly scattered when the cavalrymen appeared. This latest intelligence, along with Varnum's report, led Custer to believe his worst fear had come true: His regiment had been discovered. When word of his approach reached the village, the Sioux certainly would break up and move in every direction to avoid capture. He immediately ordered an officers' call.

Custer informed his subordinates they had been detected by the Sioux. The chances that they would now find the village intact was highly unlikely. This development forced him to change his original plan. Rather than wait until the next day to move against the Sioux, he decided to advance earlier and attack any bands they might encounter. He ordered each company commander to inspect his men and to detail parties to support 1st Lt. Edward Mathey, guarding the pack train.

Captain Frederick Benteen, commanding Company H, was the first to report back to Custer. In turn, Custer directed him to lead the advance. Once preparations were completed, the 7th U.S. Cavalry set out across the divide toward the valley of the Little Bighorn.

The regiment rode for several miles before Custer brought it to a halt around 10 a.m. Under the impression that the Sioux had split up and scattered, he decided to divide the command into battalions in an effort to engage the individual bands. Captain Benteen was given companies D, H, and K. Custer ordered him to move out to the left, to "pitch in" to anything he encountered, and to report any developments back to Custer. To Major Reno, Custer assigned companies A, G, and M. Captain Thomas McDougall's Company B was assigned rear guard. Custer himself would lead the remaining companies. As Benteen trotted away, Custer and Reno advanced.

Following receipt of Custer's message, Frederick Benteen moved to join the regiment only to encounter Reno's battalion on the bluffs. They advanced in an attempt to locate Custer's battalion, but overwhelming numbers of Sioux and Cheyenne warriors forced them back. Benteen and Reno led a stubborn defense of their hilltop position until relieved by Gibbon and Terry on June 27. Benteen served with the regiment during the Nez Perce war. He was promoted to major and transferred to the 9th U.S. Cavalry in 1882. Benteen retired in 1890 and lived in Atlanta until his death eight years later. He is buried in Arlington National Cemetery. (nps, wbnhs)

After crossing the divide, Custer and Reno advanced through Reno Creek Valley toward the Little Bighorn River. Some of the troopers briefly watered their horses in this area, known as the Morass. (dd)

They proceeded "down through a small valley" and came across a tributary of the Little Bighorn. Custer followed it, his companies on the right bank and Reno on the left, still without encountering any Sioux. About an hour after he divided the command and upon nearing the river, Custer reached a single tepee. Inside was a burial scaffold. Stopping for an inspection, one of his scouts, Fred Gerard, rode to the crest of a nearby knoll and peered across the landscape on the other side. He immediately wheeled about and yelled, "Here are your Indians General, running like devils!" This immediately caught Custer's attention.

Apparently, the Sioux were still close by but perhaps in the midst of a retreat. Despite the possible discovery of his regiment, Custer decided to launch a reconnaissance in force. Removing his hat, he beckoned for Major Reno to join him. The general already had instructions in mind when the major rode up. Through his adjutant, 1st Lt. William W. Cooke, Custer directed Reno to bring his battalion to the right bank. "General Custer directs you to take as rapid a gait as you think prudent and charge the village afterwards," Cooke said, "and you will be supported by the whole outfit." Cooke and Capt. Myles Keogh were to accompany Reno and observe his progress.

Reno's companies trotted off and disappeared from sight. Custer then "followed Reno's trail . . . some distance," remembered Sgt. Daniel Kanipe. Suddenly, Cooke and Keogh reappeared, riding fast. Reno had crossed the river, they breathlessly informed Custer, and moved on only to encounter parties of mounted Sioux.

In order to get a better understanding of the situation, Custer turned to the right and led his men up onto the hills east of the river, elevation that offered a better vantage point. Reaching the high ground, Custer stopped atop the crest of a hill. Below him, Reno was charging down the valley toward the village.

Emboldened, Custer galloped along. With an engagement taking shape, he knew the regiment would need its extra supply of ammunition. His brother Tom was at his side, and George instructed Tom to send a courier at once. The captain ordered Kanipe to ride back, find McDougall, and bring up the pack train. Ahead, Custer noticed a ridge that dropped off steeply toward the river. The bluff would give him another view of the valley. While the column came to a halt, Custer proceeded to the crest. Once again he caught sight of the village, as well as Reno, who had halted his charge and was fighting in a dismounted skirmish line. Custer paused for a few moments to assess the developing battle, and he resolved to launch a separate assault with his larger force. Wheeling about, Custer rejoined his battalion.

Sloping away from the bluff's edge on the opposite side of the ridge, Custer noticed a ravine that could provide cover as he moved to find a ford to the river. Again, Custer led his battalion on at the gallop. Before long, they entered a much larger coulee, and the pace slackened. Along with the rest of the ammunition, Custer decided he also needed the remainder of the regiment. Turning to Cooke, he ordered him to send a dispatch to Benteen. Trumpeter John Martin, an orderly, was nearby. Abruptly, Custer turned to Martin. "Trumpeter, go back on our trail and see if you can discover Benteen and give him this message." Cooke quickly scribbled out a note and thrust it toward Martin, who put spurs to his horse and left the column. The message he carried read: "Benteen. Come On. Big Village. Be quick, bring packs. W.W. Cooke. P.S. Bring pac . . . s."

Depicted here during the Civil War, Marcus Reno briefly engaged warriors on the valley floor before he withdrew to a stand of timber along the river and then retreated to the bluffs above. Criticized for his actions at the battle, Reno requested a Court of Inquiry, which ultimately cleared him of any wrongdoing. Court-martialed in 1879, he was dismissed from the army on April 1, 1880. His record was corrected in 1967 to reflect an honorable discharge. He rests today in the Little Bighorn National Cemetery. (loc)

First Charge at Catlett's Station

CHAPTER ONE

A biting early morning Virginia wind greeted the blue cavalry as it trotted along the railroad tracks. The long fingers of the winter of 1862 had extended into the middle of March. Sometimes the men could feel a touch of spring in the air, but the chilling wind only added to the loneliness of the landscape. On either side of the embankment stretched a desolate countryside, crisscrossed by ridges and swales. Ominous storm clouds hung on the horizon, which only guaranteed more misery later. It mattered little, for these men were Regulars, the professional soldiers. Rather than focus on the weather, the 5th United States and 6th United States Cavalry bowed their heads and rode on.

Around 2 p.m., officers called the 6th to a halt while the 5th U.S. rode ahead to locate the enemy. It was not long before the regiment's advance guard spotted horsemen roving about on a distant ridge. While some strained their eyes to get a better sense of the enemy's strength, a young second lieutenant checked his sidearm and made sure his sabre was near at hand. A fight was imminent.

* * *

The small boy clasped his father's hand tighter as they made their way through the village streets. It was muster day in New Rumley, Ohio, for Emmanuel Custer, a member of the local militia. His son, George Armstrong, often enthusiastically accompanied him to the town square for drill. Born in a two-story log home on December 5, 1839,

Custer led the troopers of the 5th U.S. Cavalry across this ground during the engagement at Catlett's Station. (dd)

Dedicated on June 22, 1932, this statue of Custer stands in New Rumley, Ohio, near his birthplace. Erwin Frey, a professor at Ohio State University, designed the monument. Unable to attend, Custer's widow Libbie listened to a radio broadcast of the ceremony. (dd)

"Autie," as his family and friends knew him, was the first child to survive infancy during Emmanuel and Maria Custer's marriage. Maria later bore four more children—Nevin, Thomas, Boston, and Margaret—which made for a raucous and loving household. Emmanuel provided for his growing family as the local blacksmith.

As an adult, George Custer fondly recalled his early years with a sense of gratitude to his father. "I never wanted for anything necessary," he wrote. "You and mother instilled into me principles of industry, self-reliance, honesty. You taught me the value of temperate habits, the difference between right and wrong. I look back on those days spent under the home-roof as a period of pure happiness, and I feel thankful for such noble parents."

While still a child, Autie went to Monroe, Michigan, to live with Ann Reed, Maria's daughter from her first marriage. The two had always been close and, with Ann pregnant, she needed help around the house. When Emmanuel purchased a farm outside New Rumley, Autie returned to help his father. "Despite the hard work . . . he was a leader in sports . . . exuberant, enthusiastic, with a noble, knightly countenance," recalled one of his school chums. Another friend observed that he was "mischievous and full of practical jokes; withal very plucky." At the age of fourteen, he was back in Monroe to continue his education. After two years at the Stebbins Academy, he went home to attend a normal school in preparation for becoming a teacher. Autie obtained his certificate and, for the next year, taught near his hometown. Still, it seemed he wanted more for himself.

Although the son of a Jacksonian Democrat, Autie wrote to his Congressional representative, Republican John Bingham, in late May 1856, regarding entrance to the United States Military Academy at West Point. Bingham replied that the year's selection had gone to another constituent. Autie would have to wait for the following year. Undaunted, Autie sought out and presented himself to the Congressman later that summer. Bingham was impressed with his deportment and forthright manner. Throughout the fall, Autie bided his time and supported himself by teaching at the local schools. Then in January 1857, he received the news he had been waiting for. Bingham had appointed George Armstrong "Autie" Custer to the academy.

Situated on the Hudson River in eastern New York, West Point was founded as an engineering school and was the nation's premier institution for educating military officers. Its basic tenets of duty and honor were supported by a rigid foundation of discipline. This new atmosphere based on discipline was a dramatic change to the freedom Custer was used to at home. He did not adjust well.

"Custer . . . was always in trouble with the authorities," remembered Peter S. Michie, a fellow cadet. "He had more fun, gave his friends more anxiety, walked more tours of extra guard duty and came nearer being dismissed more often than any other cadet I have ever known. Custer said that there were but two positions of distinction in the class— head and foot; and as he soon found that he could not be head he determined that he would support his class as a solid base."

Panel exhibits stand today on the foundation outline of the Custer birthplace. The house was constructed in 1817 by his maternal grandfather, James Ward. Part of the house was used as a tavern. Custer's mother, Maria, and her first husband, Israel Kirkpatrick, resided there for a brief period. Israel passed away in 1835, as did another New Rumley resident, Matilda Custer, the wife of Emmanuel Custer. Maria and Emmanuel married on February 23, 1836. Tragically, they lost their sons James and Samuel before the birth of George Armstrong. (dd)

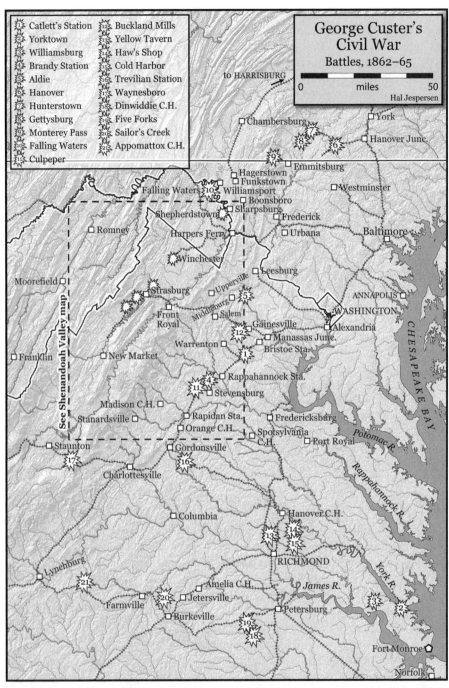

1 Catlett's Station	12 Buckland Mills
2 Yorktown	13 Yellow Tavern
3 Williamsburg	14 Haw's Shop
4 Brandy Station	15 Cold Harbor
5 Aldie	16 Trevilian Station
6 Hanover	17 Waynesboro
7 Hunterstown	18 Dinwiddie C.H.
8 Gettysburg	19 Five Forks
9 Monterey Pass	20 Sailor's Creek
10 Falling Waters	21 Appomattox C.H.
11 Culpeper	

George Custer's Civil War

Battles, 1862–65

0   miles   50

Hal Jespersen

GEORGE CUSTER IN THE CIVIL WAR—George Custer participated in a number of battles and skirmishes in the Civil War's Eastern Theater. This map indicates the location of each engagement, with the number in the star corresponding to the chronological list in the upper-left corner. The dotted-line box in the map corresponds to a map of Shenandoah Valley actions that can be found on page 96.

Infractions were tracked by a system of demerits. If a cadet accrued 200 in the academic year, he was dismissed from the academy. Over the course of four years, Custer accumulated a total of 726. In several instances, when Custer approached the maximum limit, he often buckled down and went for several months without being skinned. "My career as a cadet had but little to command it to the study of those who came after me, unless as an example to be carefully avoided," Custer wrote.

Despite his disciplinary problems, Custer's fellow cadets were drawn to his warm personality and outgoing demeanor. He was a "light hearted and gallant fellow," cadet Morris Schaff reminisced. "His nature, so full of those streams that rise, so to speak among the high hills of our being. I have in mind his joyousness, his attachment to the friends of his youth and his never ending delight in talking of his old home." James Wilson, a future Union general, observed that Custer was "a fellow of tremendous vitality and vigor" and stood "six feet tall, with broad shoulders, deep chest, thin waist and splendid legs, he had a perfect figure and was one of the best horsemen of his day."

Custer as a cadet at West Point. The coat is now on display at the Little Bighorn Battlefield National Monument. According to one of his classmates, Custer displayed an affinity for the Irish song "Garryowen" while at the academy. The tune became the official marching song of Custer's post-Civil War regiment, the 7th U.S. Cavalry. (nps, lbhbnm)

While Custer and his classmates studied and prepared to become soldiers, the world outside West Point was slowly coming apart. For decades, the issue of slavery had hung a dark pall over the country. With the election of Abraham Lincoln to the presidency in November 1860, the issue ripped the nation apart. The following month, South Carolina seceded from the Union. Mississippi, Alabama, Florida, Georgia, Louisiana, and Texas soon followed, together forming the Confederate States of America. Consequently, Southerners from each seceding state resigned from the academy.

"No one speaks of anything but war and everyone in this part of the country firmly believes that we will hear in a few days that hostilities have commenced," Custer wrote to Ann in April. "If we must have a war, I . . . have no objections to serve my country to the best of my ability." His words were prophetic. Two days later, Confederate forces opened fire on Fort Sumter in Charleston Harbor. President Lincoln responded with a call for 75,000 volunteers from the Northern states to suppress the rebellion. These green recruits would

Winfield Scott was the most distinguished American soldier of his era. (loc)

Custer's regiment was only lightly engaged at First Manassas. Along with the regular cavalry, his unit was detailed to guard the Union right flank. The 2nd U.S. Cavalry was positioned here on Chinn Ridge for part of the battle. (dd)

be in sore need of training from competent officers, which prompted Congress to reduce the five-year curriculum at West Point to four. Rather than graduate in 1862, Custer prepared early for his last examinations. When they concluded, Custer ranked thirty-fourth in a class of thirty-four.

Although he had graduated, Custer had not yet left behind his penchant for antics. One morning in June, as officer of the guard, fisticuffs between two cadets broke out in front of Custer's tent. "The instincts of a boy prevailed," he recalled. Instead of arresting those engaged, Custer emerged and shouted, "Stand back, boys; let's have a fair fight." "I had occasion to remember, if not regret, the employment of those words," he later wrote. The fracas also had attracted the attention of two other officers who made their way to the gathering, which quickly dispersed. Custer was immediately ordered to the Commandant and promptly placed under arrest. While his friends departed to join the army, he remained behind to face a court martial for failing to break up the fight. Officers, however, were in short supply and needed at the front. Custer was ultimately reprimanded in orders and soon left for Washington.

Arriving early on the morning of July 20, Custer made his way to the Adjutant General's office to receive his orders, which assigned him to the 2nd U.S. Cavalry. While there, by chance, he was introduced to General in Chief Winfield Scott. A veteran of the War of 1812 and victor over Mexico, Scott was the greatest soldier in America in 1861. Custer was completely overwhelmed when

Scott asked that he carry messages to Maj. Gen. Irvin McDowell, whose army was then outside Washington and moving against Confederates at Manassas. The young lieutenant procured a horse, picked up his dispatches, and rode out into the night to find McDowell's headquarters.

Custer reached McDowell in time to learn the Federal commander was planning an offensive on the enemy that morning and soon found his regiment. Later that day, he experienced his first action in the battle of First Manassas. "I remember well the strange hissing and exceedingly vicious sound of the first cannon shot I heard as it whirled through the air," he wrote. "I had often heard the sound made by cannon balls while passing through the air during my artillery practice at West Point, but a man listens with changed interest when the direction of the balls is toward instead of away from him."

Philip Kearny quickly earned a reputation as one of the Union army's hardest-fighting officers. (loc)

After initial Union success, Confederate reinforcements turned the tide and repulsed McDowell's onslaught. Although the Union retreat became a rout, his regiment along with the other U.S. Regulars made their way off the field in an orderly fashion. The following afternoon, they reached Arlington Heights and the safety of Washington.

Shortly after the battle, Custer was detached to serve on the staff of Brig. Gen. Philip Kearny, "a very peculiar, withal a very gallant leader," Custer recalled. He "was a man of violent passions, quick and determined impulses, haughty demeanor . . . brave as the bravest man can be." Custer did not remain long in this position as the War Department issued orders that prohibited regular officers from serving on the staff of volunteer generals. This came as a blessing to Custer. Suffering from poor health, he went back to Monroe to convalesce. He departed at a pivotal moment for the Union soldiers around the capital as Maj. Gen. George McClellan replaced McDowell after the debacle at Manassas. McClellan began to mold and fashion his men into an efficient force, which he rechristened the Army of the Potomac. The cavalry was organized under the command of Brig. Gen. George Stoneman, and Custer's regiment was re-designated as the 5th U.S. Cavalry.

Custer rejoined the army in January 1862. Like many of his comrades, he waited with anticipation for the upcoming spring campaign. "We are waiting

A native of Tampa Bay, Florida, John McIntosh served in the U.S. Navy prior to the Civil War. His brother James was a Confederate general who was killed at Pea Ridge. Cedar Run would not be the last time Custer and McIntosh fought together. (loc)

for roads in order to march," he wrote Ann. "We have had two days of fine weather and six more days like them will put us on the road . . . to victory or defeat. I am confident, however, that we will be successful in our next attempt on Manassas."

The enemy, however, would not await the Union offensive. Anticipating the Union movement, Gen. Joseph Johnston, commanding the Confederate force opposite Washington, abandoned his position in order to better protect the capital at Richmond. Early in March, Johnston began to pull his divisions out of their encampments and march south.

Curious but cautious, Federal units sallied out to investigate. "The rebels have left all of their positions," McClellan wrote to Secretary of War Edwin Stanton from Fairfax Court House on the night of March 11. "I am satisfied they have fallen behind the Rapidan to Fredericksburg and Gordonsville." To confirm this observation, McClellan dispatched Brigadier General Stoneman to ascertain Johnston's whereabouts.

* * *

Amidst dreary conditions on March 14, Custer rode out with his regiment and accompanied Stoneman. The troopers followed the line of the Orange and Alexandria Railroad south from Manassas through Bristoe Station. Some eight miles down the line, about a mile from Catlett's Station, Confederate cavalry was spotted along the north bank of Cedar Run. After several moments of observation, Custer and the rest of the officers rode to the head of the regiment to confer with their commander, Maj. Charles Whiting. Soon, an order arrived from Stoneman that directed him to push ahead and disperse the Confederates. Whiting immediately directed Custer and 1st Lt. John B. McIntosh to take their companies and attack. "I marched . . . to the front, formed line and advanced," Custer remembered. "Advancing without opposition to the base of the hill upon which the pickets were posted, when within convenient distance I gave the command 'Charge' . . . . my company responded gallantly, and away we went."

The gray cavalry responded with a volley but gave way before the Federal attack. Reaching the railroad bridge that spanned the stream ahead of Custer and McIntosh, the Confederates crossed and then set it on fire. Unable to pursue, the two officers recalled their men and returned to Whiting.

Later that evening, the regiment bedded down for the evening. Next to a crackling fire, an exuberant Custer pulled his blanket close to his chin. It was hard to sleep; thoughts of the day's engagement danced through his head. Self-assured because he had just led his first mounted assault, Custer recognized the value of his conduct. As an officer, he had the responsibility to motivate the men under him. It was one thing to direct troops into a fight, but leading them from the front was quite another. His success that day came from his own ability to inspire his troopers to follow him.

Exhaustion eventually caught up, and he drifted off to sleep.

The Confederates withdrew before the advance of Custer's and McIntosh's troopers. A correspondent with the *New York Tribune* who witnessed the action wrote, "The charge in front was beautifully made, and as the Fifth rode up the hill, the rebels took to their heels and retreated across Cedar Run, destroying the railroad-bridge by fire as they went along." The modern bridge is located in the middle distance. (dd)

PA 12

SEVEN DAYS' BATTLES
NEW BRIDGE

Leading up to and during the Seven Days' Battles from 25 June to 1 July 1862, bridges and roads played an important role in the movement of the Union and Confederate armies. New Bridge on the Chickahominy River was 1.5 miles south of here, and was one of the most important of the many river crossings. Union army troops marched through this region to Mechanicsville on 24 May 1862. Confederate Maj. Gens. James Longstreet's and Ambrose P. Hill's divisions used the New Bridge on 29 June 1862 as they moved south toward Glendale, where they fought

The Fight at New Bridge

CHAPTER TWO

Trees surrounding the riverbank trapped the humidity close to the ground. An occasional breeze provided some comfort but not enough for the two riders. One had already opened the lower buttons of his frock coat in the hopes of relief from the May warmth.

Occasionally deer darted back and forth amidst the undergrowth. Finally, the two men brought their horses to a stop along the Chickahominy River. They cast their eyes in each direction for any indication of activity. All was quiet. Brigadier General John Barnard turned to 2nd Lt. George Custer and instructed him to jump in. Custer dismounted, drew his side arm, and carefully waded into the water.

* * *

Something had stirred deep inside Custer as he led his troopers in the charge at Catlett's Station. "The bullets rattled like hail," he confessed with excitement in a letter to his parents. The feelings of nervousness and anxiety he had experienced at Manassas had been replaced with exhilaration. His naturally adventurous spirit was drawn to battle. Fear of wounds or even death did not seem to trouble Custer. In the coming days, he would have to cling to this spirit oblivious to his own vulnerability. The Army of the Potomac was on the precipice of 1862's spring campaign.

A few miles from the Gaines's Mill and Cold Harbor battlefields is a maker commemorating the engagement at New Bridge. The site along the Chickahominy River is inaccessible to the public. (dd)

Gen. George B. McClellan, commander of the Army of the Potomac, earned the admiration of George Custer. (loc)

Custer is depicted here, lying down on the right, amidst a group of fellow officers. Next to Custer may be Rose, a dog he adopted during the Peninsula Campaign. (loc)

With Johnston's withdrawal from his immediate front, McClellan planned to transfer his army from Washington down the Potomac, through the Chesapeake Bay to Fort Monroe, nearly 100 miles southeast of Richmond. Then he planned to advance up the Yorktown Peninsula and capture Richmond. Like many of McClellan's soldiers, the young Custer admired the man affectionately known as "Little Mac." "I have more confidence in General McClellan than in any man living," he wrote home. "I would forsake everything and follow him to the ends of the earth. I would lay down my life for him."

Custer and the 5th U.S. Cavalry embarked from Alexandria on March 27. After landing at Fort Monroe, they rode up the Peninsula and joined the army on April 5 at Warwick Court House, outside Yorktown, where the Confederates had been waiting for McClellan. McClellan obliged them by digging in for a siege. To supervise the construction of field fortifications, Custer was detached from his regiment and assigned to serve with the topographical engineers. He reported to 1st Lt. Nicolas Bowen, the chief engineer on the staff of Brig. Gen. William "Baldy" Smith.

"Work was carried on in the trenches during the night, their close proximity to the enemy's batteries rendering it impracticable during the hours of daylight," Custer remembered. "In the daytime other parties were employed constructing gabions and fascines, filling sandbags, and completing earthworks." Men in blue and gray remained in a near constant state of skirmishing, and Custer became adept at dodging sniper fire while on the front line. These small engagements reinforced the true cost of war in Custer's mind.

"The day before yesterday we buried our dead . . . in the clothes they wore when killed,

George Custer (left) and his constant companion through the spring of 1862, Nicholas Bowen (center). (loc)

A Civil War Trails marker within the Union fortifications outside Yorktown discusses Custer's efforts while detailed as an engineer in the spring of 1862. (dd)

One of Custer's assignments at Yorktown was supervising the construction of Union earthworks, including this covered way. It is located off a walking trail in the modern Newport News Park. (dd)

each wrapped in his blanket," he wrote to Ann on April 20. "Some were quite young and boyish, and, looking at their faces, I could not but think of my own younger brother." One of the slain made a particular impression on him. He had married his sweetheart the day before he left home. "Just as his comrades were about to consign his body to the earth, and, not wishing to put my hands in his pockets, cut them open with my knife, and found knife, porte-monnaie and ring. I then cut off a lock of his hair and gave them to a friend of his . . . who promised to send them to his wife." Amidst the drudgery of the siege, Custer remained confident. "General McClellan is here to lead us so we are certain of victory," he told his sister.

Along with these duties, Custer received an assignment he found "peculiar": he ascended in a balloon to observe enemy activity. On one of these flights in early May, he discovered the Confederates had abandoned their works near Yorktown. The Federals immediately set off in pursuit and found the gray in a new position outside Williamsburg.

On May 5, the Union army attacked. In the ensuing battle, Custer was attached to Brig. Gen. Winfield Scott Hancock's command. With Custer leading the way, the 5th Wisconsin and 6th Maine crossed a dam over Cub Run Creek. Hancock then followed with his other regiments, moving up onto high ground opposite the enemy left flank. There, Hancock held his position against repeated Confederate assaults. Custer remained close to Hancock's side throughout the fight, assisting with the positioning of artillery. Pressure up and down the gray line eventually forced the Confederates to retreat, leaving the old colonial city in Union hands.

After the engagement, Custer encountered John Lea, one of his former classmates, then a Confederate captain. Lea had been wounded in the leg. That the two men were engaged on opposite sides in a great war was overshadowed by memories of their time together at West Point. Lea burst into tears, and the two embraced. Custer brought Lea meals while he recuperated in the hospital. "I . . . gave him stockings of which he stood in need and some money," Custer wrote. "His last words to me were God bless you old boy." The experience would haunt Custer in the days ahead.

The Union victory at Williamsburg forced the Confederates to withdraw north up the Peninsula. McClellan followed. Heavy rain turned the soft soil into muck, but by May 20, elements of the army reached the Chickahominy. "At the season we struck, it was one of the most formidable obstacles that could be opposed to the advance of the army," McClellan's chief engineer, Brig. Gen. John Barnard, recalled. The last impediment between the enemy and Richmond, Johnston had ordered many of the crossing sites destroyed to impede the Federal progress. On the morning of May 23, Barnard took Custer with him to the vicinity of New Bridge to find a place for the army to ford.

Federal earthworks are still visible at Yorktown. (dd)

At Yorktown, Custer participated in several balloon reconnaissances launched from Warwick Court House. Ascending about 1,000 feet in the air, "it was a kind of danger that few persons have schooled themselves against, and still few possess a liking for," he remembered. (dd)

Custer slowly made his way across the river. Although the bottom was firm, the water was high and came up to his chest. When he reached the opposite bank—to Barnard's surprise—Custer kept going and disappeared into the woods. Scouting, he moved slowly, brushing aside branches. Suddenly, he smelled smoke. Making his way a little farther, he came in sight of an enemy picket post. Not only were they unaware of his presence, but he noticed they were located at a bend in the river and vulnerable to being attacked in the flank. After observing them for several moments, Custer returned to the river and rejoined Barnard. Custer told him what he had found, and the chief engineer decided to report directly to McClellan.

Barnard and Custer reached army headquarters just as the commanding general was departing with his staff to inspect the lines. Humbled to be so near McClellan, the young second lieutenant hung back and then fell in at the rear of the party as they passed. Custer guided his horse onward while trying to wipe the dirt from his uniform. Suddenly, the rider in front of him beckoned and said McClellan wanted to speak to him. Nervously, Custer rode ahead and saluted the commanding general, who inquired about the venture across the Chickahominy. Concisely, he explained to McClellan what he had observed. McClellan was impressed by the feat as well as by the young officer's demeanor and the clarity of his report. "Do you know that you are just the young man I've been looking for Mr. Custer?" he said. "How would you like to come on my staff?" For a moment, time stood still. "I felt I could have died for him," Custer remembered. He readily accepted.

With a ford located, McClellan decided to assemble a force to attack the Confederates. The next morning, Custer and Nicolas Bowen accompanied elements from the 2nd U.S. Cavalry and 4th Michigan Infantry down to the river. As they reached the location Custer had discovered the previous day, shouts emanated from the ranks of the Michigan regiment. "Why, it's Armstrong!" "How are you, Armstrong?" Many of the soldiers recognized Custer from his early days in Monroe.

"Well boys, I'm glad to see you; you don't know how glad," he responded. Custer also recognized the moment as a chance to inspire the men for the coming fight. "All Monroe boys, follow me; stick to me and I'll stick to you! Come!"

Quietly, a platoon from Company A of the 4th Michigan deployed near the ford while the balance of the regiment and the 2nd U.S. Cavalry waited near the bridge site. At a given signal, Custer led

After abandoning Yorktown, the Confederates fell back to their fortifications at Williamsburg. (dd)

Custer accompanied Brig. Gen. Winfield Scott Hancock's brigade at the battle of Williamsburg. "As we were about ready to start, a young lieutenant came dashing up on horseback," recalled a Wisconsin soldier of Custer. "We learned that he was a member of the 5th Regular Cavalry, serving as volunteer aide, and had been sent to lead us. His sudden appearance at once interested the men and they welcomed him with a shout. The 5th Regiment will never forget that figure or face." Hancock's infantry crossed a mill dam and advanced into the woods on the opposite side of the pond and beyond to engage the Confederates. (dd)

them out of the woods and to the river. "In the men plunged, all accoutered as they were, but contrived to keep their muskets in condition to use," wrote a correspondent from the *New York Herald* who accompanied the Federals. Once the party crossed, they moved south in conjunction with another platoon on the east bank.

Several hundred yards from the crossing, Custer and his men encountered elements from the 5th Louisiana and quickly began to roll up the enemy line. Apprised of the fighting on their left, the Tigers set fire to New Bridge. A charge by the 2nd U.S. failed to save the structure. Amidst the flames, "the balance of four companies of the Fourth Michigan were immediately thrown into the river," Bowen wrote. "Our men crossed under a severe fire." Once on the other side, they were joined by Custer and his platoon. Then "the work of firing commenced" as the 4th Michigan formed a line of battle and engaged the Louisianans.

Reinforced by the 10th Georgia, the 5th Louisiana launched several assaults, but the Wolverines held firm. "The rebels had two pieces of artillery, from which they hurled shells at our men, but the shells . . . passed over the heads of our men," observed the reporter. "The shooting continued for nearly two hours." After expending their supply of ammunition, the blue infantry withdrew to the east side of the river.

Soaking wet again, Custer rode alongside the men as they returned to their camps. Ascending a ridge, he turned back to look out across the plain toward the Chickahominy and reflected on the last two months. His efforts had not gone unnoticed. The recognition had come from a man whom Custer held in highest regard. He was overcome by a sense of accomplishment and excitement with his new assignment. Most importantly, it reinforced in his mind the lesson of Catlett's Station. Williamsburg and New Bridge proved once again that if he could inspire his men through his own actions, he could be victorious on the battlefield.

Such accomplishments, large and small, helped Custer develop confidence in his own abilities. Like his conduct, his certainty also translated to the ranks, which could help overcome fear in the most adverse conditions. Whether in the field or on staff duty, it was something Custer would remember.

The famous artist Alfred Waud produced this sketch of Custer wading the Chickahominy at New Bridge. (loc)

Friends at War

CHAPTER THREE

Candles flickered inside Bassett Hall as the last rays of sunlight disappeared below the western horizon. The light bounced across the parlor, casting the shadows of those gathered against the walls. Open doors welcomed in fresh air that brought the smell of summer flowers. On one side of the room stood a Confederate captain, resplendent in a new dress uniform of gray. Standing over his right shoulder was George Armstrong Custer.

* * *

Elevation to McClellan's staff brought a brevet rank of captain for Custer. It would not be long before he had an opportunity to make good not only on the promotion but, most importantly, the commanding general's faith in his abilities.

Eight days after the fight at New Bridge, Joseph Johnston struck the Union army near Fair Oaks. The Confederate commander was wounded in the subsequent battle. President Jefferson Davis chose his military adviser, Gen. Robert E. Lee, to succeed Johnston and defend Richmond. Lee possessed an aggressive mindset, and rather than await McClellan, he decided to go on the offensive. Lee focused on Maj. Gen. Fitz John Porter's V Corps, the only Union force on the north bank of the Chickahominy. On June 26, the Confederates attacked at Mechanicsville, northeast of the capital. Although the Union infantry held their ground, the

Likely built by Philip Johnson, a member of the House of Burgesses prior to the American Revolution, this house in Williamsburg was purchased by Burwell Bassett in 1800. Bassett was a nephew of Martha Washington. George Custer attended a wedding of a Confederate officer and former West Point classmate, John Gimlet Lea, here in the summer of 1862. (dd)

Custer, right, sits next to James Washington, a friend from West Point and Confederate officer. A relative of the first president, Washington was captured at Fair Oaks. The kindnesses extended by Custer during Washington's captivity were not lost on his family. As a token of their gratitude, they later presented Custer with a button from a uniform coat worn by George Washington.
(loc)

Federals abandoned their lines early the next morning for a stronger position south of Boatswain Creek.

The skills Custer had developed in reconnaissance earlier in the spring proved to be an advantage for him. Rather than remain at army headquarters, McClellan kept him near the front lines to serve as his eyes and ears. When Lee attacked Porter early on the morning of June 27 at Gaines's Mill, Custer monitored the fight and sent reports back to McClellan as the action developed. Around 5 p.m., Custer guided the brigades of Brig. Gens. William French and Thomas Meagher across Grapevine Bridge to reinforce Porter. That evening, Lee launched an assault that broke the enemy line and pushed the Federals back across the Chickahominy.

Lee's aggression was enough to cause McClellan to reconsider his plans of capturing Richmond in 1862. Rather than hold his ground or launch a counterattack, he elected to withdraw to Harrison's Landing on the James River and the safety of the Union Navy. Custer, along with Nicolas Bowen, remained with McClellan throughout the retreat, accompanying the Federal infantry and hounded by the enemy. Two days after Gaines's Mill, Lee struck the blue infantry at Savage's Station and again the next day at Glendale. By July 1, McClellan's infantry had assumed a position on a long, high plateau called Malvern Hill.

That morning, Custer and Bowen, accompanied by some orderlies, rode out beyond the picket lines to reconnoiter. As they approached a thicket, a group of enemy cavalrymen surprised them, approaching for the same purpose. Custer and his companions turned and galloped for safety, the Confederates close on their heels. Outdistancing their pursuers, Custer and his small party quickly wheeled about, pulled their pistols, and bore down on the Confederates. Their sudden charge stunned the gray troopers, who surrendered to a man.

Later in the day, Lee sent his infantry up Malvern Hill in an assault on the Union position. The Federals repulsed the attack and, when night fell, they abandoned their lines and set off on the last leg of their march. Around dark on July 3, the last of McClellan's men tramped into their new lines at Harrison's Landing. With the threat to Richmond alleviated, Lee decided not to assail McClellan again and was content to keep a close eye on his foe.

The lull left Custer at headquarters attending to administrative duties. He found the clerical work tedious and longed to be in the field again. The restless young officer did not have to wait long for another chance to fight.

To confirm reports of Confederate movement south of the James, McClellan sent elements from the 1st Michigan Infantry, 3rd Pennsylvania Cavalry, and the 5th U.S. Cavalry out to investigate. Custer rode along with the Regulars, accompanied by Bowen. Under the overall command of Col. William Averell of the 3rd Pennsylvania, the contingent ferried across the river. Reaching the far bank, Averell sent the 5th U.S. ahead as an advance guard, which was followed by the rest of his force.

Custer spent the first weeks of his assignment to McClellan's staff at McClellan's headquarters, the Peter Trent house. (dd)

The commander of the Army of Northern Virginia, Robert E. Lee, served briefly in the 2nd U.S. Cavalry prior to the war. It was the same regiment Custer was assigned to at the First Battle of Bull Run. (loc)

The blue cavalry had scarcely gone a mile when it ran into Confederate skirmishers. Averell deployed his men only to see the Rebels slowly withdraw back on their main line. As the skies opened, Custer pulled his kepi down over his forehead and reached for his saber as the Federals prepared to attack. With the signal to advance, he lowered the blade toward the gray coats. "The enemy gave way, and we pursued in good order as fast as we could," Averell remembered.

From prisoners taken in the engagement, Federals learned that a larger camp, laden with supplies, was just a few miles away near Sycamore Church. The initiative in hand, Averell decided to continue and sent mounted skirmishers forward. Once again, buglers sounded the advance, and the Union cavalry slammed into the Confederates, blue troopers "driving the . . . pickets before them."

"We found . . . goods, tents, commissary stores, cooking utensil, clothing &c.," wrote Averell. He promptly ordered the supplies destroyed, and the small force made its way back to the river.

Around 2 a.m. on August 5, Averell led the Pennsylvanians and Regulars out again. They marched north in support of Maj. Gen. Joseph Hooker's division in an effort to gain information regarding Confederate strength around Richmond. Custer went along as an observer for McClellan. Mid-morning found the Union troopers at White Oak Swamp Bridge. Similar to the expedition to Sycamore Church, Averell placed the 5th U.S. Cavalry in the lead, supported by the 3rd Pennsylvania. He ordered his troopers to "dash at once upon the enemy as soon as he should be discovered," and his men moved forward "with life."

Soon they encountered elements from the 10th Virginia Cavalry. The blue troopers prepared to charge, "and away we went, whooping and yelling with all our might," Custer wrote. "The rebels broke and scattered in all directions, we following as fast as our horses could go. As soon as we came close enough, we began firing at them with our revolvers. Quite a number of them surrendered when they saw that their escape was cut off."

During the fracas, Custer, along with a bugler boy, became separated from the command. Custer had lost sight of the bugler in the brush when suddenly he was alarmed by the boy's cries. Two

Confederate cavalrymen were bearing down on the lad. Custer drew his pistol and rode to his comrade's aid. At Custer's appearance, the Rebels turned and rode off. But Custer wasn't through: he told the bugler to take one of the Confederates while he chased the other. "My horse was the fastest," Custer wrote. "I kept gaining on him until I was within ten steps when I called out to him to surrender." His quarry refused and then Custer fired two warning shots, which brought him to a halt. The Virginian hesitated but then handed over his weapon to Custer, who turned and escorted his prisoner back to the regiment.

When he returned, the Regulars set out again. The scrap with the 10th Virginia had stirred up the enemy, and small parties roved about Averell's troopers. It was not long before Custer and about ten troopers ran into more Confederates, who promptly turned and retreated. As Custer and his men pursued, a gray officer caught Custer's eye, and he "selected him as my game." Custer followed the Rebel over a "stout rail fence." Similar to the incident earlier in the day, Custer called out to his adversary to surrender. This time, however, the officer paid him no heed. Custer took careful aim and fired. The shot missed, and he ordered him again to give up "but received no reply." Custer fired again, and this time the Confederate "sat for a moment in his saddle, reeled and fell to the

Union soldiers on engineering duty at Grapevine Bridge. (loc)

The Union position at Malvern Hill dominated the Confederate advance. (dd)

ground." The rest of his men reached Custer's side just as the notes of "rally" echoed through the woods. Custer broke off the chase and returned to his regiment.

Before doing so, Custer captured the horse of the officer he had killed. The saddle was "a splendid one," he wrote home, "covered with black morocco and ornamented with silver nails." "The sword of the officer was fastened to the saddle, so that altogether it was splendid trophy." Custer also managed to pick up a "splendid" double barreled shotgun, which he later sent home to his brother Boston. Shortly after Custer joined the main force, the 1st North Carolina Cavalry appeared on the scene. These enemy reinforcements prompted Averell to withdraw to the Federal lines.

Although McClellan had dispatched various scouting missions, the rest of his army remained idle, passing the months of July and August in camp. This inactivity, along with the way McClellan conducted himself in the recent battles with Lee, frustrated both General in Chief Henry Halleck and President Abraham Lincoln. On the same day that Custer set out with Averell in the Sycamore Church expedition, Halleck, fed up with McClellan, ordered him to evacuate Harrison's Landing at the beginning of August and head north. The Army of the Potomac slowly began to make its way back to Fort Monroe for transport. Custer joined the rest of the headquarters staff as they journeyed south along the Peninsula.

The march brought Custer back to Williamsburg. Sight of the old battlefield brought back memories of the May engagement. Custer had been haunted by his encounter with John Lea and subsequently learned that Lea had been exchanged and returned to the city. Custer made inquiries about him to the locals and was eventually directed to the house where Lea was staying. "I immediately visited him and was rejoiced to find him almost recovered from the effects of his wound," Custer wrote. "He was surprised and glad to meet me." Despite being dressed in Union blue, Custer was welcomed into a house that was "secesh." The two friends spent several hours in conversation. As their talk ended, Lea made him promise to come back and spend the night.

Custer immediately made his way back to camp, received permission from McClellan to return, changed his clothes, and arrived at the house again just in time to enjoy a hearty dinner. In the company of "two beautiful young ladies," the two foes gathered around the piano to serenade everyone. Lea then pulled Custer aside and informed him was engaged to the elder of the two women. "He was anxious that I should be present at his marriage," Custer recalled. He was shocked at the request. The man across from him was his enemy, who, if they met on the battlefield, would attempt to take his life. Custer and Lea, however, had shared the experience and rigors of West Point together. Their instruction on the drill field and in the classroom as well as long hours of study all while yearning for home had forged a friendship between them. Even though they now wore different uniforms, the bonds forged at West Point could not be broken. For Custer, this made the answer simple. "I replied that I would like to do so but I feared I could not remain so long," he wrote. After some discussion, Lea and his bride resolved to conduct the ceremony the following evening in order for Custer to attend.

Custer stayed with his former classmate most of the next day and only returned to camp long enough to get into his dress uniform. Around 9 p.m., the ceremony commenced. "It was a strange wedding," Custer confessed. "We had been warm friends at West Point. . . .[W]e were both struck by

In early August, Custer accompanied Brig. Gen. William W. Averell on two scouting missions. (loc)

During a skirmish at White Oak Swamp, Custer captured a sabre made of Damascus steel from a Confederate officer. On it was a Spanish inscription that, translated, states, "Do not draw me without cause; Do not sheath me without honor." It is now on display at the Little Bighorn Battlefield National Monument. (dd)

the strange fortune which had thrown us together again, and under such remarkable circumstances." An Episcopal minister presided as the couple exchanged vows and then were pronounced man and wife. The meal that followed was "excellent and passed off very pleasantly." In the morning, Custer rode to rejoin McClellan, only to find he had left the city. Custer promptly sent a telegram, and McClellan responded that he could remain in Williamsburg if he chose.

Custer so chose, staying with the new couple at Lea's father-in-law's for nearly two weeks. "Every evening was spent in the parlor," Custer wrote. "We were all fond of cards and took great interest in playing. 'Muggins' and 'Independence' were the usual games, sometimes euchre."

Despite the peaceful respite, Custer could not escape the bitter reality of the situation. He was cast in a conflict that found him and his friends on opposite sides. Late one night, Custer gathered his belongings and thanked his gracious hosts. Then he shook hands with Lea, stepped out of the house, and mounted his horse. Lea remained in the doorway. Custer grimly saluted his enemy, turned his horse's head and rode off. Not saying a word, he headed back to war.

Like Custer, Lea would also eventually ride away from Bassett Hall. Despite wounds at Chancellorsville and Third Winchester, he eventually rose to brigade command. (dd)

Across Beverly Ford

CHAPTER FOUR

After only a few hours' rest, officers roused blue cavalrymen from their blankets. After feeding horses, the regiment mounted and made its way quietly to the ford. Although sunrise was only a few minutes away, a dense fog hung in the air. The soldiers carefully guided their mounts through the mist to the river. One officer whispered commands at the bank. Another watched intently, his eyes darting to the far side and then back again as the column began to cross. First Lieutenant George Armstrong Custer waited for several more minutes, then turned his horse to carefully guide it into the water. When he reached the far bank, Custer looked back to inspect their progress. Then somewhere up ahead, a shot rang out. He peered ahead to see muzzle flashes through the trees. First one, then another and yet another—the fire rising in a crescendo until the air was filled with the sharp reports.

*   *   *

The transfer of the Army of the Potomac north left Custer absent from the army longer than he'd expected. Finally, though, the time had come to return to duty. After he left Williamsburg, he made his way to Yorktown where he learned that McClellan had already departed for Alexandria. Custer continued to Fort Monroe, boarded a boat to Baltimore, then took a train to Washington to reunite with his commander.

Much had transpired in his absence. While McClellan had vacated the Peninsula, Lee had moved his Army of Northern Virginia north to

In the opening phase of the battle of Brandy Station, Custer accompanied Col. Benjamin "Grimes" Davis's command as it crossed the Rappahannock River and advanced along the Beverly Ford Road. (dd)

Custer spent much of the battle of Antietam at McClellan's headquarters rather than in the field serving as the eyes and ears of the army commander. For years, historians believed the Pry House served as McClellan's HQ, although recent scholarship has thrown that into doubt. (dd)

confront a new threat from a Union army under Maj. Gen. John Pope. At the end of August, Lee engaged Pope near the old Manassas battlefield and soundly defeated the Federals. On September 2, the remnants of Pope's army were combined with the Army of the Potomac with McClellan in overall command.

In the wake of his victory over Pope, Lee decided to carry the war beyond the Potomac and invade the North. In response, McClellan lumbered out of the Washington defenses and into Maryland, establishing his headquarters in Rockville. Custer, who had remained in the city, rode in the company of his fellow staff officers to meet him.

From Rockville, the Federals moved on to Frederick. There, by a stroke of brilliant luck, Union soldiers found an order lost by a Confederate staff officer. The order outlined the position of Lee's forces along with his intentions for the campaign. In response, on September 14, McClellan sent his columns west toward South Mountain, where enemy infantry guarded the passes. After a brutal fight, Union infantry from the I and IX Corps broke through. At dawn the next morning, Brig. Gen. Alfred Pleasonton, in command of the army's cavalry division, set out with the 8th Illinois in pursuit of the enemy. Similar to his field duties on the Peninsula, Custer accompanied Pleasonton.

"After passing the summit of South Mountain and descending into the valley, we found almost every house and barn converted into a hospital for Rebel soldiers," wrote a Union cavalryman. Confederate cavalry waited for Pleasonton in the village of Boonsboro. The Illinoisans charged into the village and, after withstanding an enemy counterattack, pushed the Confederates out of the town. "Thus for a distance of two miles was kept up a running, hand to hand fight," wrote a member of the 8th Illinois, "until the rebels had scattered on different roads and through fields, making further pursuit unavailing." During the engagement, Custer remained with Pleasonton, pried intelligence from Confederate prisoners, and kept in contact with McClellan.

Once the Federals had gained control of the surrounding countryside, Custer rode beyond Boonsboro to Keedysville. He continued another two miles until he reached the banks of Antietam Creek. On the other side of the stream, Custer found the Confederates "drawn up in a line of battle on a ridge." He studied the enemy position for a time before he returned to the Union line.

Two days later, McClellan attacked Lee along Antietam Creek. In the face of superior numbers, Lee managed to hold on and repulse the Union assault. However, with the initiative gone, he decided to abandon his position and return to the safety of Virginia.

Surprisingly, throughout the engagement, rather than send Custer to observe the battle,

Following the battle of Antietam, President Abraham Lincoln visited the Army of the Potomac in Maryland. Lincoln stands at center, opposite McClellan. Custer stands at the far right, outside the group of officers. (loc)

McClellan kept his aide near headquarters. Little Mac may have recognized a paradoxical characteristic in Custer: While he was resourceful and a valuable member of the staff, Custer craved the excitement and thrill of combat. Such a trait could be dangerous as it compelled Custer to always be where the fighting was the most ferocious. Shortly after the battle, Custer confessed in a letter to his cousin, "I must say that I shall regret to see the war end. I would be willing, yes glad, to see a battle every day during my life. Now do not misunderstand me. I only speak of my own interests and desires perfectly regardless of all the world besides." Custer had come to believe he had been built for war.

Although he had managed to push Lee off Northern soil, caution overtook McClellan, who was slow in pursuing the Confederates. By the time the Federals reached Warrenton, Virginia, in the first week of November, President Lincoln had had enough of McClellan's vacillating. He relieved him of command of the Army of the Potomac and replaced him with Maj. Gen. Ambrose Burnside.

McClellan's removal reverted Custer to first lieutenant and left him without an assignment. Distraught and in despair with the situation, Custer took a furlough to travel home to Monroe. It would not be long before his outlook changed for the better, though. While attending a party later that month, he was introduced to the daughter of a local judge, Elizabeth Clift Bacon. Custer was instantly smitten. Suddenly, all of his anguish disappeared in that moment. "Libbie," as friends and family called her, was intelligent and vivacious. She had captured the young officer's heart, and Custer soon became a regular caller at the Bacon home. However, Daniel Bacon, Libbie's father, disapproved of his daughter socializing with the young officer. While the Custers and Reeds managed to make a decent living, they were not included—as

When he returned to the army in the spring of 1863, Custer was assigned to the staff of Brig. Gen. Alfred Pleasonton. He is mounted here on the left opposite Pleasonton. A member of the West Point Class of 1844, Pleasonton had served in the 2nd U.S. Dragoons before the war. He commanded a cavalry division during the Antietam and Fredericksburg campaigns before he was elevated to corps command after Chancellorsville. (loc)

the Bacons were—in the ranks of Monroe's elites. Libbie was smitten with the handsome, long-haired cavalryman but was forced to break off contact with him. Still, he managed to keep in contact with Libbie through winter social engagements.

Custer returned to the army for several days in December, but was soon back in Monroe. Without an assignment, he remained on leave through the early months of 1863. Then in early April, he left Monroe and traveled to Washington. Before his departure, Custer and Libbie decided to stay in contact and correspond through a mutual friend, Nettie Humphrey.

Custer was not in the capital long. McClellan had requested his assistance in compiling the official reports from the previous year's campaigns. The former army commander found the process to be a "tedious, difficult & disagreeable task," and he welcomed Custer's help. Together, the two men labored away in McClellan's Manhattan residence to complete the reports for submission to the War Department.

One of Joseph Hooker's most impactful contributions to the Army of the Potomac was to consolidate all of his mounted units into a corps under a sole commander. (loc)

On April 13, Custer received orders to report to the 5th U.S. Cavalry in Washington. His old company had lost its commanding officer, and Custer was recalled to fill the vacancy. First mustering his men in the city, Custer then leisurely marched south. After a five-day journey, he reached Stafford County and the Army of the Potomac on May 5. The next day, he was assigned to Alfred Pleasonton's staff.

Custer returned to a command where "gloomy" and "discouraging" only began to describe the situation.

* * *

On May 21, 1863, Custer and a small force of cavalry embarked on the *Caleca* and *Manhattan* down the Potomac to the Yocomico River. Making its way overland, the party reached Urbana on the Rappahannock. There, Custer burned two enemy schooners and captured twelve Confederates and thirty horses before safely returning to Federal lines. (dd)

While Custer had enjoyed his leave, Burnside had been soundly whipped by Lee in December at Fredericksburg. His successor, Maj. Gen. Joseph Hooker, did not fare any better. Despite a promising start to the spring campaign, he fell victim to Lee's maneuvering at a crossroads west of Fredericksburg known as Chancellorsville. This disaster brought recriminations throughout the Union high command. One of the men blamed for the defeat was Maj. Gen. George Stoneman, the head of the Federal Cavalry Corps, whom Hooker replaced with Pleasonton.

Lee was inspired by his twin victories and, like the previous summer, resolved to "transfer . . . hostilities north of the Potomac." Such a movement, he reasoned would offer a better opportunity to engage the Federals and, at the same time upset their plans. Lee's first task was to order his vaunted cavalry under Maj. Gen. James Ewell Brown "Jeb" Stuart to assemble in Culpeper County in preparation for screening the infantry march. Operating along the north bank of the Rappahannock River, Brig. Gen. John Buford's Union cavalry soon discovered the enemy concentration on the other side of the river. Under the assumption that Stuart was about to embark on a massive raid toward Washington, Hooker directed Pleasonton to attack the Confederates. The Union cavalry chief planned for two columns to cross the river, unite at a nearby railroad stop called Brandy Station, then move on Culpeper and defeat Stuart.

Custer's assignment was to ride with Buford during the expedition. In anticipation of the movement on the night of June 8, Custer stole a few moments to scribble a letter to Ann. "We have just taken our supper. The General has gone to sleep. The rest of the officers are lying around wrapped in their blankets. I am 'Officer of the Day' and must remain awake most of the night. . . . [A]s to myself, I never was in better spirits

By the early summer of 1863, the Confederate cavalry under Maj. Gen. James Ewell Brown "Jeb" Stuart had established its dominance over its Federal counterparts. Stuart had conducted several mounted expeditions around and behind the Union lines with little resistance from the Union cavalry. This tide would begin to shift at Brandy Station. (loc)

The Confederate Horse Artillery had bivouacked in this field on the morning of June 9, 1863. The Beverly Ford Road is marked by the tree line. Grimes Davis was killed in the road at the upper left center of the picture. (dd)

than I am at this moment." While Custer yearned for battle, it seemed that he also recognized the dark specter that accompanied it. He then directed that "in case anything happens to me, my trunk and other articles should be sent to Monroe. . . . I want all my letters burned."

A little after 4 a.m. on June 9, Custer met one of Buford's brigades, directed by Col. Benjamin Davis, near its crossing at Beverly Ford. Custer was accompanied by a bugler named Joseph Fought. After they reached the opposite bank, the two rode along until gunfire erupted at the front of the column. Davis's lead regiment, the 8th New York, had encountered pickets of the 6th Virginia Cavalry from Brig. Gen. William Jones's brigade. The New Yorkers pressed through the Virginians' line and galloped on. "There were two or three Rebels near the woods, but we clipped along toward them, and they fired at us," Fought wrote. The two men quickly returned fire. "One kept on . . . the other got back to the woods."

Davis led his troopers up and out of the river bottom along the Beverly Ford Road. Approaching a bend, a lone Confederate officer surprised Davis and shot him dead.

Buford's advance, however, had shocked the Confederate cavalry. Stuart was encamped around Brandy Station, not Culpeper as Pleasonton had believed, which allowed Stuart to quickly feed men into the fight. As the battle escalated, additional regiments from Jones's brigade arrived and steadily began to push back the blue horsemen. "The 8th New York had broken and retreated," the bugler remembered. "Our regiment had rushed to the stone wall, knowing the thing to do was to hold it. Lt. Custer and I put spurs to our horses at the same moment, expecting to go down any minute. My horse took the wall, but the Lieutenant was long-legged and his horse not large, and he fell in going over, but was up again immediately." Fortunately, Custer was not injured, and the two men rode off and reported to Pleasonton.

Jones's determined stand bought time for Stuart's other brigades to reach the scene. Stuart anchored his new position on a ridge that bore the name of a local house of worship, St. James Church. Custer found his chief with Buford atop a high knoll near the Union right. Intimidated by Stuart's opposition and his formidable line, Pleasonton was content to allow Buford to skirmish and exchange artillery fire with the Confederates. Late in the morning, though, word reached Stuart that Brig. Gen. David Gregg's division had appeared in his rear. Gregg had crossed the Rappahannock downstream at Kelly's Ford and, as he reached the battlefield, was poised to deal a devastating blow,

A member of the 8th New York Cavalry recalled the thick undergrowth that lined the Beverly Ford Road. (dd)

trapping Stuart between his force and Buford. In response to this threat, Stuart skillfully pulled brigades from the St. James Church line to send them back to engage the Federals. A new front opened along high ground that rose above Brandy Station, a ridge called Fleetwood Hill.

Despite the Union onslaught, Stuart managed to hold on both fronts. As the sun began to set, Pleasonton ordered Buford and Gregg to withdraw across the Rappahannock. Begrimed with sweat and dirt like the other troopers, Custer accompanied Pleasonton as they trotted back to Beverly Ford and up the north bank. "There could not be a prettier sight," recalled a fellow staffer. "The river flowed beneath us; as far as we could see to right and left on the southern bank no living object was visible; the plain and woods in front of us were growing misty, but the burnished and glowing horizon threw everything on high ground into wonderful relief."

Custer's conduct during the fight had impressed the Union cavalry commander. He ordered Custer to take the captured flag of the 12th Virginia Cavalry to present to Hooker.

After a night's rest and breakfast, Custer started out for army headquarters with several other cavalrymen. A pleasant morning, it promised to grow hot. Custer had become accustomed to Southern summers, and rising temperature did not dampen

After the opening phase of the battle, Stuart consolidated his troopers along St. James Church Ridge, which runs along the distant tree line. (dd)

John Buford and Alfred Pleasonton observed and directed the fighting from this knoll. (dd)

his spirits. He had not participated in a battle since Boonsboro the previous September, but in his return to the battlefield, he had performed well and had once again caught the eye of his commander.

The distance created by his sojourn since McClellan's removal was gone. Confident and determined once again, he was finally back where he belonged: with an army in the field. Riding along, his thoughts turned to the days ahead and the next major battle.

$$\mathcal{A} \ New \ \mathcal{B}rigadier$$

CHAPTER FIVE

Tired men wiped sleep from their eyes as the column wound its way past the many cornfields that dotted the countryside. Some grumbled as they rode, disgruntled after being rousted from their bivouac. Their complaints were met with icy stares from sergeants and corporals, causing the grumblers to button up.

Reaching an intersection, the men turned to the left. They could see, ahead in a small group, astride his horse, their commanding officer. Binoculars in hand, he surveyed the surrounding area. Turning to members of his staff, George A. Custer motioned and pointed, and the aides galloped off. Squadrons rode away in every direction to reconnoiter. Riders came and went, bringing in reports. All was quiet, but Custer still felt uneasy.

Slowly, the hours passed. Then, a large plume of smoke burst forth from the far ridge, and a shell came screaming down into the midst of Custer's position.

* * *

Dedicated on June 18, 1889, the Michigan Cavalry Brigade monument stands at Gettysburg. In attendance at the ceremony was the former commander of the 5th Michigan Cavalry, Russell Alger, and Michigan's Governor, Cyrus Luce. James H. Kidd of the 6th Michigan delivered the keynote address. Custer led charges by the 1st and 7th Michigan over the field where the monument now stands. (dd)

Custer's actions at Brandy Station had given him the honor to present the captured battle flag to Joe Hooker. He wasted little time returning to the cavalry commander, though. In the days afterwards, he returned to Pleasanton, who had pulled the cavalry back to Warrenton Junction. There, for the next several days, he continued to monitor the situation and report his findings to

Alfred Waud sketched Custer at the head of the 1st Maine Cavalry at Aldie. (fw)

Joseph Hooker. Something was clearly afoot with Lee's army, and four days after the engagement at Brandy Station, Hooker ordered his army to march north, along the Orange and Alexandria Railroad, to cover Washington and be in a better position to respond to an enemy movement. Custer rode with Pleasonton to the vicinity of Manassas Junction.

Hooker, however, was becoming suspicious of Pleasonton's efforts. The army commander still lacked concrete information regarding Lee's whereabouts or intentions. In the early morning hours of June 17, Hooker sent a terse dispatch to Pleasonton. "The commanding general relies upon you with your cavalry . . . to give him information of where the enemy is. . . . [Y]ou have a sufficient cavalry force to do this." It was clear Hooker was not happy with him. By sunup, Pleasonton had David Gregg's division in the saddle, headed out in search of Lee.

Custer accompanied Gregg as the Federals rode west on the Little River Turnpike. East of Aldie, one of Gregg's brigades under Brig. Gen. Judson Kilpatrick ran into elements of Col. Thomas Munford's command. Kilpatrick steadily gained the upper hand, pressing the Confederates back through Aldie and soon controlling the village. The fighting then shifted to the north, where Munford held a stone wall along the Snickersville Turnpike.

Repeated assaults by Kilpatrick failed to dislodge the enemy. An emboldened Munford launched a counterattack.

This Confederate assault threatened to capture Capt. Alanson Randol's Battery E/G, 1st U.S. Artillery on a knoll near the intersection of the turnpikes. With a crisis near at hand, Kilpatrick turned to the 1st Maine Cavalry and directed directed it to charge. Custer had remained near Randol throughout the engagement. When Kilpatrick ordered the Mainers forward, he could not help but join in. Drawing his sabre, Custer spurred his horse to the front of the regiment. The 1st Maine slammed into Munford's Virginians, and the ensuing melee pushed them back to the stone wall. Darkness finally brought an end to the fighting.

Like Custer, George G. Meade also had a quick rise to command in the spring of 1863. One of the better division commanders in the Army of the Potomac, Meade was elevated to command the V Corps prior to the Chancellorsville campaign. President Abraham Lincoln elevated Meade, although junior in rank to his peers, to army command at the end of June. (loc)

Pleasonton continued to put pressure on Stuart's cavalry. Over the course of the next four days, fighting erupted west of Aldie at Middleburg and Upperville. Although Stuart continued to fall back to the west, he kept Pleasonton away from the Blue Ridge Mountains, which helped screen the Army of Northern Virginia as it moved through the Shenandoah Valley. Custer remained at Pleasonton's side throughout these engagements before moving with his chief to Leesburg and then across the Potomac to Poolesville. From there, they moved on to Frederick.

Hooker had done well in managing the march from the Rappahannock to Maryland. Still, he remained under the dark cloud of Chancellorsville, and the Union high command had grown weary of him. Late in June, after quarrelling with Halleck, Hooker was replaced with the head of the V Corps, Maj. Gen. George G. Meade. Pleasonton took the opportunity to approach his new commander on the subject of elevating three officers to the rank of general and incorporating a division of cavalry serving in the Washington defenses into the Army of the Potomac. Meade acquiesced: Wesley Merritt, Elon J. Farnsworth, and George Armstrong Custer were all promoted to brigadier general. Farnsworth and Custer were given brigades in the new 3rd Cavalry Division, which was now led by Judson Kilpatrick. This meteoric jump in ranks was unheard of. These young officers

In late June, Alfred Pleasonton made his headquarters north of Frederick at Richfield. It was here that Custer was informed he had been promoted to brigadier general. The house depicted was reconstructed on the original site. (dd)

were to lead others who were not only twice their age but had more experience. Additionally, they would be issuing orders to subordinates who, until Pleasonton's unprecedented request, were senior in rank to them.

The cavalry chief wanted officers "whom he knew" in command, but more importantly, he made the bold move because he wanted "gallant" leaders that would make their men "brighten up" on the battlefield. He recognized that Custer had this quality. Catlett's Station had taught Custer that success came from inspiring those in the rank. He had refined this ability at New Bridge, and it had become part of his personality. The trait had also been on display at Brandy Station and Aldie.

On the afternoon of June 28, 1863, as Custer lounged about headquarters north of Frederick, Pleasonton called him inside. Custer sat in Pleasonton's room as he received the news of his promotion and momentarily forgot where he was. Scarcely believing his ears and thinking he would burst, Armstrong stood up, grabbed Pleasonton by the hand and managed to stammer his thanks. Beaming, he could not help but run out of the house. He had much to do.

Custer was to lead the Michigan Cavalry Brigade, which consisted of the 1st, 5th, 6th, and

7th Regiments. His brigade was also augmented by Battery M, 2nd U.S. Artillery under Capt. Alexander C. M. Pennington. If Custer would not have enough firepower at his disposal with Pennington's guns, the 5th Michigan and two companies from the 6th Michigan were armed with new Spencer seven-shot repeating rifles.

Custer first went to find bugler Joseph Fought. Armstrong had never dressed well, considering his duties, but now he needed a uniform befitting his new rank. Together, the two men put together Custer's new set of clothes. Early the next morning, Custer set out in the direction of the Mason-Dixon Line at the head of the 1st and 7th Michigan to rendezvous with the other regiments who had been scouting in the Keystone State while on the march.

Custer moved on to Littlestown, where he bivouacked for the evening. The next day, Custer and the rest of Kilpatrick's division headed east toward Hanover. Passing through, Kilpatrick and Custer had turned toward Abbottstown. The column came to a halt when shots rang out from the direction of Hanover. Farnsworth's brigade had run into Brig. Gen. John Chambliss's Confederate cavalry. Chambliss constituted the vanguard of a force under Jeb Stuart. Since the battle of Upperville, Stuart had led Chambliss, along with the brigades of Brig. Gens. Fitzhugh Lee and Wade Hampton, in a ride around the Army of the Potomac and through Maryland.

Despite the surprise, Farnsworth rallied and drove the gray cavalry out of Hanover. Custer soon

On June 21, 1863, Pleasonton once again dispatched Custer to accompany David Gregg's division. Custer fell in with the 6th Ohio Cavalry as the regiment entered the engagement at Upperville. An Ohio trooper recalled, "In the afternoon of that day, we reached Upperville, and here I first remember General Custer, then a captain, and perfect type of the dashing cavalryman. Our line was formed on the right of the road, on the side of the hill, on whose opposite slope was the town of Upperville. Here, Custer, taking two companies from our left, charged into the town to draw out the enemy in pursuit, upon which the remaining companies were to charge his flank, and gain an easy victory. Soon back came the two companies, Custer, with his long flaxen hair flying in the wind calling out: 'Here they come boys.' 'Forward!' was the order, and on we dashed, saber in hand. (dd)

A Civil War Trails sign at Richfield tells the story of "The Boy General of the Golden Locks." (cm)

Upon his arrival at the Hanover town square, Custer tied his horse to a maple tree that had been planted by local merchant Josiah Gitt in 1860. The tree was removed in 1924, but a gold star in the sidewalk, surrounded by four horseshoes, marks the spot where the tree stood (left). A plaque explaining the story of the "Custer Maple" is mounted on a building nearby (right). (dd) (dd)

arrived and, fortunately, found that the fighting had drawn the attention of the 5th and 6th Michigan, which eventually arrived from Littlestown. He found them near the town's railroad depot. As Stuart's cavalry deployed south of Hanover, Custer ordered his men to dismount and move to engage them. "I heard a voice new to me, directly in rear of the portion of the line where I was, giving directions," recalled the 6th Michigan's Capt. James H. Kidd:

> *Tall, lithe, active, muscular, straight as an Indian and as quick in his movements, he had the fair complexion of a school girl. He was clad in a suit of black velvet, elaborately trimmed with gold lace, which ran down the outer seams of his trousers and almost covered the sleeves of his cavalry jacket. The wide collar of a blue navy shirt was turned down over the collar of his velvet jacket, and a necktie of brilliant crimson was tied in a graceful knot at the throat, the long ends falling carelessly in front . . . a soft, black hat with wide brim adorned with a gilt cord, and rosette encircling a silver star . . . his golden hair fell in graceful luxuriance nearly or quite to his shoulders, and his upper lip was garnished with a blonde mustache.*

Following some brief skirmishing, Stuart decided to break off the fight and withdraw to rejoin Lee. Kilpatrick also pulled out and resumed his march to Abbottstown. On July 2, he was directed to ride west. The day before, Lee and Meade had engaged at the south-central Pennsylvania town of Gettysburg. The 3rd Cavalry Division was needed there to cover the army's right flank.

Custer's brigade led the advance. Passing through the small village of Hunterstown, less than six miles from Gettysburg, the 6th Michigan ran into a party of gray cavalrymen. Outnumbered, the Confederates gave way before the Wolverines. The young general soon galloped to the head of the column, which had reached a low ridge outside of Hunterstown. In the growing twilight, he spotted the enemy below, now in retreat. Custer drew his sabre, turned to those around him, and yelled, "I'll lead you this time boys. Come On!" The Wolverines charged after the Confederates and right into the teeth of Hampton's brigade. Custer had stumbled upon Hampton's rear guard, the Cobb's and Philips's Legions.

George Custer's velveteen jacket now hangs on display at the Little Bighorn Battlefield National Museum. (lbhbnm)

Both sides met in a sharp bend in the road. Slashing away at the butternuts, Custer felt a jolt and he tumbled to the ground, his horse shot from

Custer's horse was shot out from under him at the bend of the road west of Hunterstown. (dd)

under him. Leaping to his feet, he was quickly picked up by one of his orderlies, Sgt. Norvill Churchill of the 1st Michigan. The Federals turned and galloped back to the ridge with the Confederates in close pursuit. Farnsworth had reached the field during Custer's little foray, and the Federals managed to repulse the enemy attack. Hampton broke off the fight soon after and withdrew under the cover of dark. Around 11 p.m., Kilpatrick led his tired division southwest and camped at Two Taverns.

Kilpatrick's division stirred early from its bivouac on July 3 and headed for Gettysburg, a little over five miles away. As the division got underway, one of David Gregg's staff officers arrived with instructions for Custer to move the brigade southeast of Gettysburg and patrol the Union right. About 10 a.m., Armstrong reached the intersection of the Hanover and Low Dutch Roads. Custer recognized the importance of the junction, for whoever controlled it had an open route to the Baltimore Pike, a road Meade would have to use should the Army of the Potomac be forced to retreat. Armstrong immediately dispatched parties to scout the area and report back on any enemy activity.

Capt. Thomas Jackson's Charlottesville Horse Artillery deployed here on Cress Ridge. In the artillery duel that preceded the fighting at East Cavalry Field, the first shot from Alexander Pennington's battery entered the muzzle of one of Jackson's guns, disabling it. (dd)

Studying the terrain to his left and toward Gettysburg, Armstrong noticed a stream, Little's Run, which ran perpendicular from the Hanover Road toward high ground about a mile northwest of the intersection called Cress Ridge. At its foot was a house and barn owned by John Rummel. Other houses also dotted the landscape. Custer soon secured the area and waited. It was not long before a breathless rider reined up and reported the approach of Confederate cavalry. That morning, Stuart, reinforced by Brig. Gen. Albert Jenkins's brigade, under Lt. Col. Vincent Witcher, had marched around the Confederate left in the hopes of engaging the blue cavalry and wreaking havoc in the Union rear. When he reached Cress Ridge, Stuart ordered several artillery shots to be fired in the direction of the road junction.

David M. Gregg directed the Union effort on East Cavalry Field. In the years since the battle, Custer's role has been inflated and, unfortunately, Gregg's contribution has been overshadowed. Gregg remained in command of the 2nd Cavalry Division until his resignation in February 1865; the reason for his mysterious resignation remains a matter of debate for historians and scholars. (loc)

Stuart's appearance was not the only thing that alarmed Custer. He had received a directive from Kilpatrick ordering him to return to the division. David Gregg was to assume Armstrong's position. Gregg soon trotted into view with one of his brigades, led by Col. John McIntosh. Custer rode over and reported on the situation. He told Gregg that he would be in a "big fight." Gregg responded that if that be the case, he wanted Custer to stay. "If you will give me an order to remain I will only be too happy to do it," Armstrong replied, and Gregg acquiesced.

Shortly after 2 p.m., his deployment complete, McIntosh sent forward squadrons from the 1st New Jersey, 3rd Pennsylvania, and elements of the Purnell Legion toward the Rummel Farm to develop Stuart's position. They were met by elements of Witcher's brigade. "From behind the stone walls, taking advantage of every ditch and little inequality in the surface of the ground, the dismounted cavalry poured forth the contents of their carbines," remembered a New Jersey trooper. Pennington, along with Randol's battery, joined in the attack, sending shells into the Confederate ranks and into the woods on Cress Ridge. Custer observed the fight from a distance. When Federal ammunition began to run low, he ordered the 5th Michigan in to relieve their comrades.

The 5th Michigan met part of Chambliss's brigade, which had moved forward to relieve

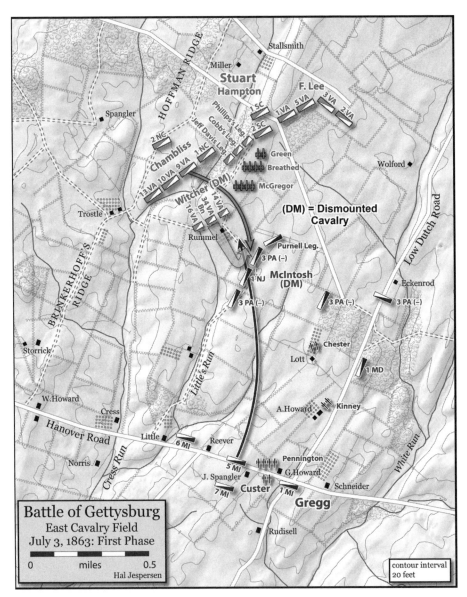

Battle of Gettysburg
East Cavalry Field
July 3, 1863: First Phase

0   miles   0.5
Hal Jespersen

contour interval
20 feet

GETTYSBURG EAST CAVALRY FIELD, FIRST PHASE—The initial phase of the fighting on East Cavalry Field was dismounted. Troopers fought for control of the John Rummel farm at the base of Cress Ridge.

Witcher. Outnumbered, Custer's regiment nonetheless held its ground, due in part to being armed with the Spencers. Depleting its own supply of ammunition, the regiment began to fall back. Seeing this, Stuart sent the 1st Virginia Cavalry in a charge against the 5th Michigan. Observing the retreat of the regiment and the developing enemy attack, Gregg ordered Custer into the fight.

Nearby, mounted in a column of squadrons, was the 7th Michigan. Galloping to their front, Custer drew his sabre, turned in the saddle and

The 5th Michigan Cavalry engaged enemy cavalry through these fields on the John Rummel farm. While the stone house is not original, the white barn was a witness to the battle. (dd)

yelled, "Come on You Wolverines!" Emboldened by their new brigadier, they went forward at a full gallop. "The ground over which we had to pass was unfavorable for the maneuvering of cavalry but, despite all obstacles, this regiment advanced boldly to the assault, which was executed in splendid style," Custer fondly remembered.

"We went . . . at a break-neck charge, down into the pithole of death into a corner of a stone wall with a fence on top of it," wrote Capt. George A. Armstrong of the 7th Michigan. "We crashed against the stone wall, which withstood us, breaking our columns into jelly and mixing us up like a mass of pulp. 'Throw down that fence!' was ordered, and the rails flew in all directions, clearing an opening for us to pass . . . through the gap in the fence our brave boys went pell-mell." Even with their momentum slowed, the 7th Michigan slammed into the 1st Virginia and bought time for the 5th Michigan to reach safety. Then, the 9th Virginia and 13th Virginia came to the aid of their sister regiment and threatened to overwhelm Custer. Fortunately, a battalion from the 5th Michigan joined the fight and held off the Virginians long enough for the 7th Michigan to return to its position.

After two hours of fighting, a disturbing silence fell over the field. Suddenly along Cress Ridge, the Confederates appeared. "In close squadrons, advancing as in review, with sabres drawn and glistening like silver in the bright sunlight, the spectacle called forth a murmur of admiration," recalled a Pennsylvanian. Stuart had launched his grand assault. Lee and Hampton pushed rapidly ahead, bent on sweeping away all that stood before them.

In response to this advance, Gregg ordered

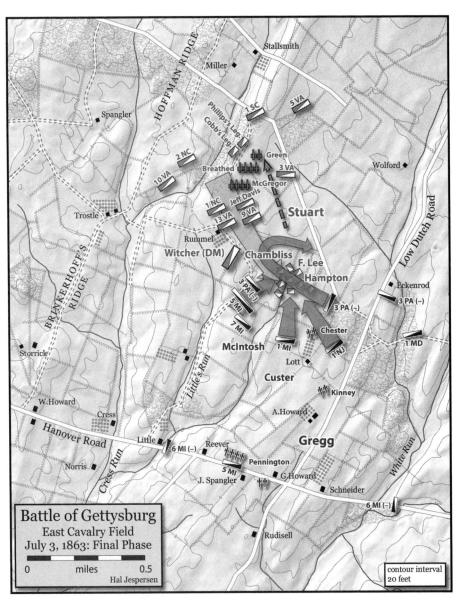

Battle of Gettysburg
East Cavalry Field
July 3, 1863: Final Phase

0   miles   0.5
Hal Jespersen

contour interval
20 feet

**GETTYSBURG EAST CAVALRY
FIELD, FINAL PHASE**—The
final phase at East Cavalry
Field consisted of traditional
mounted charges and hand-to-
hand combat.

the 1st Michigan to attack. Shortly after receiving
the directive, Custer rode to the head of the
regiment. Once again, he drew his sabre, and "the
gallant body of men" rode forward. "They first
came on in walk, then took the trot," Pennington
remembered. "My six three-inch guns, and
Randol's four Napoleon, poured a withering fire."
Clearing the muzzles of his artillery and now in the
open, Armstrong ordered a charge and with "a yell
that spread terror before them," the 1st Michigan

crashed into the gray horsemen, "sabering all who came within reach."

Following the initial impact of the Wolverines' attack, elements from the 1st New Jersey, 3rd Pennsylvania, and 5th Michigan joined in the assault. "For a moment, but only a moment, that long heavy column stood its ground," Custer wrote. "Then, unable to withstand . . . our attack, it gave way." Stuart's cavalry retreated to Cress Ridge. Peering down, the gray cavalier did not attempt another attack and, late in the day, returned to the main Confederate line.

Around dark, with the Hanover and Low Dutch Road intersection secure, Custer was ordered back to Two Taverns. Riding along at the head of his Wolverines, he removed a gauntlet to wipe the sweat from his brow and his face. He was tired and struggled to keep from falling asleep in the saddle. His exhaustion, however, could not overcome a sense of gratification. Over the course of the last four days, he had fought in three major engagements. Prior to his promotion, Custer had never led a force numbering more than 100 men. Nor had he benefitted from the mentorship and tutelage of a senior officer in the field. His brush with death at Hunterstown aside, Custer's performance was not only shocking but remarkable.

His feelings were suddenly tempered with caution. An uncertain future lay ahead.

$\mathscr{B}$uckland $\mathscr{M}$ills

CHAPTER SIX

The men consumed the last sips of coffee and rinsed their tins in the nearby stream. They kicked out their fires, crammed their last bits of hardtack into their mouths, and then mounted. All was ready, and the Union cavalrymen set out once again along the turnpike. Ahead lay open fields on both sides, lined by woods on their far edges. To cover the march, Brig. Gen. George A. Custer dispatched the 6th Michigan to the south and directed them to fall in once the brigade had passed. Together with his staff, Custer rode on in the lead.

All seemed quiet, save for the sound of horseshoes striking the road. Custer trotted on, keeping a close eye on the woods. Suddenly, gunshots rang out behind him. An officer galloped up from the 6th Michigan with news that enemy cavalry had been spotted.

*   *   *

The original abutments for the bridge that spanned Broad Run on the Warrenton Turnpike near the village of Buckland Mills still stand today next to the modern highway. (dd)

On Independence Day, Custer, along with the rest of Kilpatrick's division, departed Two Taverns and headed toward Emmitsburg, Maryland. Meade had defeated Lee at Gettysburg, and the Confederate army was in retreat. Kilpatrick was to meet Col. Pennock Huey's brigade from Gregg's division and then pursue a Confederate wagon train. Sadly, Custer's fellow newly minted brigade commander would not participate in the hunt. Elon Farnsworth had been killed the day before when Kilpatrick had ordered an ill-advised charge on the southern end of the battlefield.

Near the Old Waynesboro Tollhouse at Monterey Pass, Companies A and C of the 1st Ohio Cavalry broke through the Confederate position. (dd)

Although a driving rain had begun to fall, Kilpatrick wasted little time after the rendezvous, and the Union cavalry turned back toward the Pennsylvania border. "It poured and poured," wrote a Michigan officer, "the water running in streams off the horses' backs, making of every rivulet a river and every river and mountain stream a raging flood." Night descended as the Federals neared South Mountain.

Upon their approach to Monterey Pass, Kilpatrick learned from a local that the Confederates had posted an artillery piece just ahead, supported by some 20 troopers from Capt. George Emack's company of the 1st Maryland Cavalry. Emack's graycoats guarded the eastern face of the mountain while wagons and ambulances from Lt. Gen. Richard Ewell's Second Corps rolled along to the west. About midnight, Emack opened fire on Custer, who led the advance. Custer immediately called a halt and ordered his men to dismount. The 5th Michigan formed to the left of the road, the 6th Michigan on the right, and their sister regiments in reserve. Custer ordered an advance, and the Wolverines went forward. Aided by the darkness, bad weather, and reinforcements from the 4th North Carolina, Emack managed to hold off several assaults.

Because of poor conditions and difficult terrain, Custer was not anxious to press the attack. Kilpatrick, however, grew impatient and ordered up the 1st West Virginia Cavalry. He ordered its commander, Maj. Charles Capehart,

At Falling Waters, the Michigan Brigade attacked Maj. Gen. Henry Heth's division positioned on the ridge to the left. (dd)

to support Custer. Arriving on the scene, Capehart prepared to charge. Custer opened the ranks to allow the West Virginians to pass. The Union cavalry stormed ahead and crashed into Emack's position, stampeding the Confederates. Kilpatrick added more weight to the assault, sending in his headquarters escort, Companies A and C, 1st Ohio Cavalry. Noticing the reinforcements in the darkness, Custer rode over to Capt. Noah Jones of the Buckeye squadron. Shaking his hand, Custer said, "Do your duty and God bless you."

"Such unearthly screaming was never heard among those old mountains," wrote one Ohio trooper as they surged ahead. Realizing he could still have an effect on the outcome of the fight, Custer drew his sabre and charged with them. As at Hunterstown, his horse was shot out from under him—but the assault broke the Confederate line, and gray troopers streamed down the opposite side of the mountain and into Ewell's wagons. Kilpatrick's division captured much of the train along with some 1,300 prisoners, who were sent on to Frederick.

Custer deployed Pennington's guns on the slopes of Battle Mountain near Newby's Crossroads. (dd)

Although tired and weary, the Michigan Brigade did not have time to rest. The Army of Northern Virginia was in full retreat, headed toward the Potomac. Over the course of the next several days, Kilpatrick's division and the Wolverines skirmished, fighting Jeb Stuart's cavalry at Smithsburg, Hagerstown, and Boonsboro. Because the rain-swollen river delayed his withdrawal, Lee set up a defensive position that stretched for more than nine miles from Downsville to just above Hagerstown—and waited. Finally, on the night of July 13, the crossing began. Early the following morning, the 3rd Cavalry Division left its bivouac at Hagerstown to reconnoiter Lee's position only to find the Southerners had vacated it. Word soon arrived that a Confederate force was still on

Custer briefly established his headquarters at Hartwood Church in August 1863. "The inhabitants have long been without sugar, coffee and salt," Custer wrote of the locals, "and for these they exchange butter, milk, eggs and vegetables. Ladies young and old whose husbands are in the rebel army come flocking to Headquarters, their little baskets of produce on the arm." (dd)

the Maryland side, though, several miles away at Falling Waters. Kilpatrick immediately turned the column "in hot haste" and galloped off.

A squadron from the 6th Michigan led the way, followed closely by Custer and the rest of the regiment. Finding the enemy works still occupied upon his arrival, Custer ordered the squadron to dismount and advance. Kilpatrick immediately countermanded the directive, ordering the troopers back in the saddle and forward. This sudden charge surprised Brig. Gen. James J. Pettigrew's North Carolina brigade, but the Tarheels soon rallied and pushed the Federals back. Custer watched as his men streamed for the rear. Reacting quickly, he formed the 1st and 7th Michigan on foot and pushed them into the fray. The Wolverines went up and over the entrenchments, driving into the Confederates, many of whom surrendered. Despite his efforts, Kilpatrick had done little to impede the enemy withdrawal, and Lee safely reached Virginia.

The day after Falling Waters, Kilpatrick went on sick leave. Farnsworth's death left Custer as the senior brigadier, so he took over in Kilpatrick's absence. Custer led the troopers across the Potomac and on to Purcellville, on the eastern side of the Blue Ridge Mountains. Over the next several days, Custer sent patrols toward the gaps to collect intelligence on the Confederates, who were

Custer's brigade crossed the Rappahannock here at Kelly's Ford during the Union reconnaissance to Culpeper Court House. (dd)

Custer sports his trademark sailor's shirt in this engraving taken from a photograph in October 1863. (b&l)

marching from the Shenandoah Valley toward Culpeper. Custer monitored their progress, steadily moving south on the eastern side of the mountains in conjunction with the enemy movement. About daylight on July 24, with five regiments and two batteries, Custer left Amissville to head toward Newby's Crossroads.

About a mile away from the junction, Custer encountered the enemy. Captured soldiers told him Lt. Gen. James Longstreet's First Corps lay just ahead. Custer set out to verify the information only to encounter Confederate infantry. So, he ordered Alexander Pennington to unlimber on the side of a mountain and open fire to develop the enemy strength. Unable to advance farther, Custer decided to withdraw. Suddenly, Col. Henry Benning's Georgia brigade, along with the 4th and 15th Alabama infantry struck Custer's left flank. Benning, nicknamed "Rock," threatened to capture the 5th and 6th Michigan along with a section of Pennington's guns. Calmly and skillfully, Custer deployed the remainder of his guns and engaged the soldiers from the Deep South. With no immediate escape route for the two regiments, Custer ordered a road cut through "a dense woods," opening a way to safety. His command united, he "deliberately" withdrew to Amissville. Unbelievably, he only lost fifteen men during the engagement. Custer had just displayed skill in extricating his troopers from a precarious position in the face of a superior enemy force.

As July turned to August, Lee assumed a position below the Rapidan around Orange Court House. Meade remained north of the Rappahannock around Warrenton. After Kilpatrick's return, Custer and the Michigan Brigade guarded the army's left. The Wolverines were responsible for picketing the countryside around Hartwood Church, and then it moved to the vicinity of Berea Church and Falmouth, just opposite Fredericksburg. In the middle of the month, the 1st Vermont temporarily joined the unit to help offset its recent losses. Along with this addition, Custer designated the band from the 7th Michigan to be the brigade band. The band's main purpose in battle was to remain close to Custer and play inspiring airs to encourage the men.

Around noon on September 12, Custer and the Wolverines stirred from their camp at Berea Church and headed up the Rappahannock. Kilpatrick, along with Brig. Gen. John Buford's division, was to move over the river in a reconnaissance in force toward Culpeper Court House. Custer bivouacked at Kelly's Ford that night and crossed the following morning. With the 5th Michigan in the lead, he headed in the direction of Brandy Station to join Buford. Waiting for them was Confederate artillery under Capt. William McGregor and a lone gun from Capt. Roger Chew's battery. Kilpatrick deployed 1st Lt. Jacob Counselman's Battery K, 1st U.S. Artillery to engage them. Buford's arrival prompted the Confederates to withdraw toward Culpeper, their retreat covered by Brig. Gen. Lunsford Lomax's brigade.

Pushing ahead, Custer sent the 5th and 6th Michigan to the left of the town where they encountered Lomax, who had been reinforced by Col. Richard Beale. Custer deployed the 7th Michigan to contend with gray sharpshooters along Mountain Run. "I dismounted 100 men with carbines, who wading and swimming the stream, charged rapidly up the hill . . . the sharpshooters retiring before them," wrote the regiment's colonel. Gaining the upper hand, Custer led the 1st Vermont in a charge through the streets. Along with the 2nd and 5th New York from Col. Henry Davies's brigade, the Federals captured Culpeper.

Fleetwood Hill was the epicenter of the June 1863 battle of Brandy Station. In the fall of 1863, the cavalry returned. Custer joined John Buford's division here after his charge against Fitz Lee's division at Brandy Station. (dd)

Judson Kilpatrick was hard enough on his subordinates that he earned the ignoble nickname "Kil-Cavalry." (loc)

Stuart's quick abandonment of high ground above the barrier of Broad Run at Buckland Mills alarmed Custer. One of the original bridge abutments stands in the center of the picture. (dd)

Kilpatrick pursued the Confederates south of town, where the gray cavalry reformed on a high ridge. When the Southerners repulsed an attack by the 5th New York, Custer led the 1st Vermont and 7th Michigan forward. Galloping ahead, an enemy shell ripped into his foot and another killed his horse. After being helped up by his aides, he was taken back to Culpeper.

There, he encountered Alfred Pleasonton. "How are you," Custer asked the corps commander before putting in a pitch for "fifteen days leave of absence." Indicating his wounded foot, he added, "They have spoiled my boots, but they didn't gain much there, for I stole 'em from a Reb." Although painful, the injury was not serious. Nevertheless, Pleasonton granted his former protégé's leave request.

*   *   *

Custer welcomed the brief respite in Monroe where he was hailed as a celebrity. Again, he attended a number of social events, mainly to see Libbie. Even with his promotion, Judge Bacon still did not approve of Libbie's contact with Custer. Still, the two were in love. After a local dance that stretched into the early hours of September 29, Custer proposed and Libbie accepted. Until Custer had an opportunity to speak with the judge, the engagement had to remain secret. His leave coming to an end, Custer returned to Virginia.

Fitzhugh Lee, nephew of Robert E. Lee, was Custer's nemesis at Buckland Mills. Wounded at Third Winchester, Lee would serve as governor of Virginia after the war and receive a commission as major general of United States volunteers during the Spanish-American War. (loc)

He found the Army of the Potomac encamped about Culpeper and the Michigan Brigade near James City. Lee stood across the Rapidan River at Madison Court House. Custer's promotion, wounding, and engagement had given him a lot to reflect on during the long hours on the train. "I think of the vast responsibility resting on me, of the many lives entrusted to my keeping, of the happiness of so many households depending on my discretion and judgement—and to think that I am just leaving my boyhood makes the responsibility greater," he wrote Nettie Humphrey on October 9. "I try to make no unjust pretensions. I assume nothing I know not to be true. It requires no extensive knowledge to inform me what is my duty to my country, my command. . . . 'First be sure you're right, then go ahead!' I ask myself 'Is it right?' Satisfied that it is so, I let nothing swerve me from my purpose."

This sense of purpose would soon be tested again. A day after writing Nettie, Jeb Stuart struck Custer's picket line. His attack was part of a larger offensive. Lee planned to attack the Union army and regain the line of the Rappahannock. Meade, however, withdrew across the river to guard his supply line, the Orange and Alexandria Railroad. Kilpatrick's division covered the army's march, and Custer fell back upon Culpeper. Leaving the 7th Michigan to monitor an enemy movement, he turned the brigade north. Soon after his departure, Stuart, in command of Wade Hampton's division, appeared and began to press the regiment back.

The two Confederate divisions threatened not only to prevent a junction between Kilpatrick and Buford but cut the Federals off from the river. "This was the situation to try the stoutest hearts," remembered a trooper in the 5th New York. Custer ordered Pennington's battery to unlimber and engage the enemy while he reinforced the 7th Michigan, and Kilpatrick deployed the Wolverines and Davies's brigade in column of squadrons. Custer removed his hat, handed it to an orderly, and rode to the head of the 1st and 5th Michigan. He yelled to his men that they were surrounded and had to open the way with their sabers. "They showed their determination by giving three hearty cheers," he wrote. Custer then turned to the band and ordered them to strike up "Yankee Doodle". The charge broke through the Confederate ranks and, together, Buford and Kilpatrick made it over the Rappahannock and out of the grasp of Stuart's cavalry.

At Buckland Mills, the Wolverines briefly held this ridge before pulling back to the north bank of Broad Run. (dd)

Over the next few days, Custer marched north, guarding the flank and rear of the army. On October 14, elements from Lt. Gen. A. P. Hill's Third Corps attacked the Federals at Bristoe Station. After a sharp fight, Hill was repulsed, and the Army of the Potomac moved on to a defensive position along Bull Run. Not willing to throw his men against the enemy fortifications, four days after the battle Lee turned back toward the Rappahannock. That afternoon, Kilpatrick put his division in motion from the village of Groveton. The Union cavalry soon encountered Stuart with Hampton's division and slowly drove them south along the Warrenton Turnpike. That night, Custer bivouacked around the village of Gainesville.

At daybreak, the Union advance resumed. Custer took the lead with the 6th Michigan driving elements of Col. Pierce M. B. Young's brigade toward Broad Run. "The stream was deep and difficult, spanned at the pike by a stone bridge," Major Kidd wrote. Young retreated across it in the face of Custer's advance. On a low ridge beyond, Stuart formed his artillery and opened fire, one shot striking so close to Custer and his staff that they frantically scattered for safety. Custer formed his brigade on the north bank and prepared to give battle. Then, to his surprise, Stuart broke off the fight and rode off. Custer led his men over the bridge to the small village of Buckland Mills and came to a halt. Davies followed behind and, at Kilpatrick's direction, set out after Stuart. When he ordered Custer to follow, Custer refused; his men had yet to eat breakfast, and he wanted to rest the horses. He had also grown weary of Kilpatrick. Thoughts of his commander's impulsive actions at Gettysburg, Monterey Pass, and Falling Waters danced through Custer's head. The division commander relented and spurred away to join Davies.

Custer justifiably was disturbed as he watched Davies disappear from sight. Stuart had given up the high ground so easily because it was all part of his plan to trap Kilpatrick. The Confederate cavalryman had planned to lure the Federals in the direction of New Baltimore. Lee's division, operating to the east, would then move beyond Kilpatrick's flank and cut off the Union cavalry from the bridge at Broad Run. After a brief meal, the Wolverines started out in Davies's wake. As a precaution, Custer dispatched Kidd to cover the left flank. It wasn't long before Lee's division appeared, and Kidd dispatched the regimental adjutant to find his brigade commander. "The Confederates displayed a line of dismounted skirmishers that ended far beyond both flanks of the regiment and a swarm of them in front," Kidd remembered.

Custer galloped back to find Kidd and then assessed the situation. He immediately deployed one of Pennington's guns on his left, which was supported by the 1st Vermont. Pennington's remaining pieces remained behind the line with the 1st Michigan in reserve. Custer formed the 5th and 7th Michigan on his right. Lee "pressed forward his dismounted line, following it closely with mounted cavalry," Kidd wrote. Custer directed Pennington to open fire with his entire battery, the "destructive fire" flying over the heads of the troopers.

Custer observed the enemy movements and quickly discerned that Lee was trying to press around his right toward Broad Run. He ordered the 6th Michigan to keep up a steady fire as Pennington limbered up. The horse artillerists whipped and cursed as the teams took off at a run to the bridge. Once on the north bank, Pennington deployed and opened fire again, this time to cover the brigade's movement. With the 6th Michigan continuing to blaze away, the other regiments pulled out of line, mounted, and moved to join Pennington.

George Custer (left) benefitted immensely from the mentorship of Alfred Pleasonton (right), who did much to advance Custer's career. Here, they were photographed together in Warrenton, Virginia, in October 1863. (loc)

The 1st Michigan was the last across. His brigade reunited, Custer slowly withdrew toward Gainesville. Lee followed but broke off the pursuit once the blue cavalry reached the village.

This sketch by Alfred Waud depicts Custer, at left center, directing his artillery at Buckland Mills. (loc)

Davies was also able to make his escape. When Custer's guns opened, he turned and headed back toward Buckland Mills. Finding it in enemy hands, Davies diverted north, crossed Broad Run above the turnpike bridge, then made for Haymarket. At Thoroughfare Gap, Davies engaged elements from Lee's division but managed to repulse an enemy assault. Abandoning his position, he continued on until he reached Custer at Gainesville.

The next day, Custer took stock of his losses. During the retreat, the Confederates had captured his trains, including his personal wagon. More wrenching was the loss of an entire battalion of the 5th Michigan, which Kilpatrick had detached without Custer's knowledge prior to the beginning of the battle. Frustrated and with a heavy heart, he found some paper and a pencil to write Nettie and Libbie: "Under very distressing circumstances I turn to you and her for consolation. It is for others that I feel . . . I cannot but regret the loss of so many brave men."

Yellow Tavern

CHAPTER SEVEN

An ominous silence fell across the woods and fields. While the gunfire had ceased, the flurry of human activity could still be heard. Amidst these sounds, a lone rider carefully made his way through a skirt of woods. He used one hand to brush aside branches as he peered across an open plain that rose to a high ridge. Putting field glasses up to his eyes, he caught sight of the enemy battery that had annoyed him a few minutes before. If several regiments could make it across the field, they stood a chance of capturing the artillery. Satisfied with what he saw, George Custer gingerly left the woods and galloped back to the Union line.

* * *

Following the disaster at Bristoe Station, Lee withdrew his army more than 20 miles to the south bank of the Rappahannock River. On November 7, Meade forced his way across the river with attacks at Rappahannock Station and Kelly's Ford. His line broken, Lee withdrew another 15 miles and took up a new position below the Rapidan River. Meade soon followed. In temporary command of the 3rd Cavalry Division, Custer drew the assignment of patrolling the area between Raccoon Ford and Morton's Ford along the Rapidan to divert enemy attention away from the infantry movement. After Lee occupied a strong position behind Mine Run, Meade determined not to risk an assault, and the

The 1st Michigan Cavalry, 7th Michigan Cavalry, and 1st Vermont Cavalry charged up this trace of the Telegraph Road to attack Jeb Stuart's position at Yellow Tavern. The Stuart monument stands to the left of the road, behind the rail fence. (dd)

After their wedding and honeymoon, Custer brought his new bride to his headquarters, Clover Hill, near Stevensburg, Virginia. (dd)

In late February 1864, Custer led a makeshift force into central Virginia as a diversion to the famous "Kilpatrick-Dahlgren Raid" against Richmond. This sketch depicts Custer's rear guard withdrawing from the vicinity of Charlottesville. (loc)

army withdrew and went into winter quarters outside Culpeper Court House.

While leading his men across Central Virginia in the closing months of 1863, events in Custer's personal life took an exciting turn. Judge Bacon had finally agreed to allow him to correspond directly with Libbie in October, and the two began to make wedding plans. On February 9, 1864, the couple was married in the Monroe Presbyterian Church. After a honeymoon at West Point, Custer took his new bride back to winter quarters in Virginia. Libbie found herself quite enthralled with life in the winter quarters. "Such style at these army dinners!" she exclaimed in a letter home. "Genl. Pleasonton has 6 courses. . . . [W]e took a lovely ride to a signal station. . . . [T]he white tents . . . stretched as far as the eye could see. . . . [O]n Sunday Custer had one of the regimental chaplains talk to the men and the band played hymns."

Shortly after this change in Custer's life, the Union war effort changed dramatically, too. At the beginning of March, Lincoln promoted Ulysses S. Grant to lieutenant general and gave him command of all the Federal armies. Coming from the West, Grant decided to direct operations while accompanying Meade's army. Grant brought with him Maj. Gen. Philip H. Sheridan, who replaced Alfred Pleasonton at the head of the Cavalry Corps. "He impresses me very favorably," Custer wrote to Libbie, who had left for Washington late in the month. Further upheaval came when Judson Kilpatrick was transferred. His impetuousness throughout the previous year and, most recently, in a failed raid on Richmond had soured his superiors on his abilities. Grant wanted someone he was familiar with from his time in the West and so brought Brig. Gen. James Wilson to take Kilpatrick's place. Custer was senior in rank to Wilson, so his brigade was transferred to Brig. Gen. Alfred Torbert's 1st Division.

Sheridan's aggressive nature fit well with Custer's command style. The bandy-legged Irishman, however, clashed with Meade on the fundamental use of the mounted arm. While Meade believed the cavalry should be employed in picketing and scouting, Sheridan felt his horsemen could better serve the army as a strike force. This disagreement remained at the surface as Grant, Meade, and Sheridan all made their preparations for the coming campaign.

* * *

As spring spread across Virginia, the Potomac army stirred from its winter's rest. In the first week of May, the Federals once again headed across the Rapidan to engage Lee. Grant and Meade planned to flank Lee's position and move beyond Mine Run into open country. Custer and the Michigan Brigade headed to Stony Mountain and then to Ely's Ford on the Rapidan on the morning of May 5. "His great height and striking countenance made him a very imposing figure," wrote an officer in the 1st U.S. Cavalry after observing Custer as his Wolverines got under way. "His blue eyes, blond moustache and great mass of blond curling hair . . . gave him the appearance of one of the Vikings of old."

Lt. Gen. Ulysses S. Grant enabled major changes to the Union cavalry. (loc)

After fording the river, the troopers moved on and encamped on the old Chancellorsville battlefield. Meanwhile, several miles away amidst the region of thick, secondary growth known as the Wilderness, Lee surprised the Union army. A pitched battle erupted along the Orange Turnpike and Brock Road/Orange Plank Road intersection. The next morning, Custer took his brigade south to a point below the Federal left along the Brock Road. There he engaged gray cavalry throughout the afternoon. With the assistance of Col. Thomas Devin's brigade, Custer managed to hold his position and that night bivouacked at Catharine Furnace.

In two days of brutal fighting, Lee once again brought a Federal advance to a standstill. Rather than retreat, though, Grant ordered the army to resume their original flanking movement and move to Spotsylvania Court House. Meade gave Sheridan's cavalry the assignment of leading the Union advance and clearing Brock Road, the main route to the Federal's destination. Custer rose early on May 7 and led the Wolverines down the Furnace Road and then turned south. "The enemy was encountered in heavy force about three-fourths of a mile beyond the cross-roads," he wrote. "A portion of the First Michigan was dismounted and advanced through the woods on both sides of the

Maj. Gen. Philip H. Sheridan was instrumental in reshaping the Army of the Potomac's cavalry corps from its traditional role into a mounted strike force. (loc)

road, while [the] remainder . . . moved up the road mounted. After a short but severe engagement the enemy were driven back."

While Sheridan managed to push Jeb Stuart's cavalry beyond the tavern, the gray horsemen still held Brock Road. When Meade arrived on the scene that night, he was infuriated to find his cavalry camped around the tavern. He immediately ordered an advance, but the troopers ran into stiff resistance. Despite support from Maj. Gen Governeur Warren's V Corps, Meade was unable to break through.

Stuart's delaying action bought time for Lee to shuffle his First Corps from the Wilderness and block the way to Spotsylvania. When Meade summoned Sheridan to headquarters for an explanation on his inability to secure the Union route of advance, their differing feelings on the utilization of the cavalry finally boiled over. The two men blew up in a profanity-laced shouting match. Then to everyone's shock, Sheridan claimed that he could "whip Stuart" if Meade gave him the opportunity. When Meade approached Grant regarding the incident, the general in chief surprisingly decided to allow Sheridan to make good on his boast. Grant told Meade to issue order for the entire cavalry corps to prepare for an expedition to engage the Confederates.

Sheridan's cavalry rendezvoused along the Orange Plank Road east of Chancellorsville and set out the next morning. The cavalry chief ordered

Custer, all his troopers now armed with Spencer repeaters, and supported by Pennington, to lead the corps with this firepower. The head of the 1st Division—commanded by Wesley Merritt while Torbert was on sick leave—marched east and then south on the Telegraph Road. "There is nothing particularly exciting or delightful in thumping along at a trot in a cavalry column," wrote an officer in the 7th Michigan. "The clouds of dust, sent up by thousands of hoof-beats, fill eyes, nose, and air passages, give external services a uniform, dirty gray color, and form such an impenetrable veil, that for many minutes together, you cannot see your hand before you."

Constructed by the Fredericksburg Iron and Steel Manufacturing Company in 1837, Catharine Furnace manufactured iron ore. During the Mexican War, it produced artillery ammunition. A key landmark on the Chancellorsville battlefield, Custer bivouacked here and ordered the furnace destroyed during the battle of the Wilderness. Only a stone stack remains. (dd)

Custer stopped for a breather at Chilesburg and then turned southeast toward the North Anna River. The Union march, however, had not gone unnoticed by the Confederates. Major General Fitzhugh Lee reported Sheridan's movement to Stuart not long after it commenced. Stuart's response was to withdraw Lee's division, which consisted of the brigades of Brig. Gens. Williams Wickham and Lunsford Lomax, from the line at Spotsylvania and set out in pursuit. Further augmenting this force was Brig. Gen. James Gordon's brigade from Maj. Gen. W. H. F. Lee's division.

As Custer reached the North Anna, his advance guard reported the presence of "a train of the enemy's ambulances" on the opposite bank at Beaver Dam Station on the Virginia Central Railroad. Custer immediately dispatched a battalion from the 1st Michigan. The Wolverines not only took possession of the rail stop but liberated hundreds of Union soldiers on their way to Confederate prison camps. "The trains were heavily laden with supplies," Custer wrote. "We captured an immense amount of army supplies, consisting of bacon, flour, meal, sugar, molasses, liquors and medical stores; also several hundred stand of arms, a large number of hospital tents, the whole amounting to several millions of dollars' worth. After supplying my command with all the rations they could transport, I caused the remainder to be burnt. I also caused the railroad track to be destroyed for a considerable distance." Custer then bedded down for the night.

Temperatures rose on May 10, and dust choked the air. Custer rode on and crossed the

Constructed in 1835, Todd's Tavern once stood in this field. On the morning of May 7, 1864, Custer advanced south along the Brock Road in the direction of this location. The tavern remained until 1884. (dd)

South Anna River at Ground Squirrel Bridge. A relentless pace had brought Sheridan within striking distance of Richmond, and Stuart would have to give battle before Sheridan reached the city's defenses. In anticipation of a fight, Custer's tired brigade was given a rest. Colonel Devin's would lead the advance the following day.

The gray cavalier was indeed planning to engage Sheridan. Stuart had also ridden hard in an effort to catch the rear of the enemy column, but Sheridan had too much of a head start. Instead, Stuart decided to let him go while he rode well to the east and then south in the hopes of cutting off the Federals. After a brief halt at Taylorsville, Stuart continued through the early morning hours of May 11 to reach the intersection of the Telegraph and Mountain Roads around 10 a.m., some six miles north of Richmond. Nearby stood a building that had long fallen into disrepair. Known as "Yellow Tavern," it had once been a wayside stop for weary travelers.

Lomax's brigade formed along Telegraph Road, facing west toward the Mountain Road and the direction of Sheridan's approach. Wickham was posted to the north along a ridge and at a right angle to Lomax's line, which was supported by Capt. William Griffin's Baltimore Light Artillery. As the Federals attacked Lomax, Stuart planned to bludgeon them in the flank with Wickham's brigade. Not long after Lomax deployed, Devin's troopers hove into view.

Merritt oversaw the deployment of his division. Devin assumed the right, Col. Alfred Gibbs the center, and Custer the left. Custer placed the Wolverines in two lines: the 5th and 6th Michigan, he directed to fight on foot; while the 1st and 7th

A reconstructed depot now stands at Beaver Dam Station. (dd)

Michigan, he held in reserve. As Merritt sent his line forward, Custer's troopers received a "heavy fire," remembered Col. Russell Alger of the 5th Michigan. Griffin's battery also lent its support and enfiladed the Union line. Combined with carbine fire on the left, the Michigan advance came to a brief halt. Then "quicker than it takes to tell it, Custer appeared," Kidd wrote. Custer ordered one of Alger's battalions to change front to deal with the threat. The 5th Michigan renewed its advance and pressed in on the Confederate line. On the right, the 9th New York from Devin's brigade had managed to turn Lomax's left. Outnumbered and with his line giving way, Lomax withdrew to reform on Wickham's left.

The 1st Virginia Cavalry held this section of Stuart's line during the battle. (dd)

Custer took advantage of the lull to reconnoiter the new Confederate position. As he studied and noted its features, he also noted a stream at the far edge of the field, at the base of the ridge. While this might slow the advance, Custer felt undeterred as he shared his findings with Merritt and Sheridan. Custer proposed to assail the center and right with the 5th and 6th Michigan. Elements from Col. George Chapman's brigade of Wilson's division, which had reached the front, would support. The main thrust would focus on Griffin's artillery. For this he would send the 1st and 7th Michigan forward in a mounted charge. A battalion of the 1st Vermont would augment the advance. Merritt agreed, and Custer formed for the attack.

An officer in the 7th Michigan watched nearby as "the 1st Michigan, in column of squadrons . . . wheeled upon my flank as a pivot with beautiful precision, and came to a halt a little in advance of me squarely in front and in full view of the Rebel guns. . . . [T]his splendid body of horsemen was halted but for a moment, when General Custer reined in at the head of it with an order to charge, and away it went toward the guns. It was swallowed up in dust and smoke. . . . [T]he earth shook, and it was evident that a besom of destruction was sweeping over the face of nature." The regiment "advanced boldly," Custer wrote, "and when with 200 yards of the battery, charged it with a yell that spread terror before them."

Reaching the crest of the ridge, the 1st Michigan struck the 1st Virginia and the Baltimore

This monument to Jeb Stuart stands within thirty feet of the spot where he was mortally wounded. In attendance at its dedication in June 1888 was one of Stuart's subordinates, Fitzhugh Lee, and Stuart's widow, Flora. (kb-d)

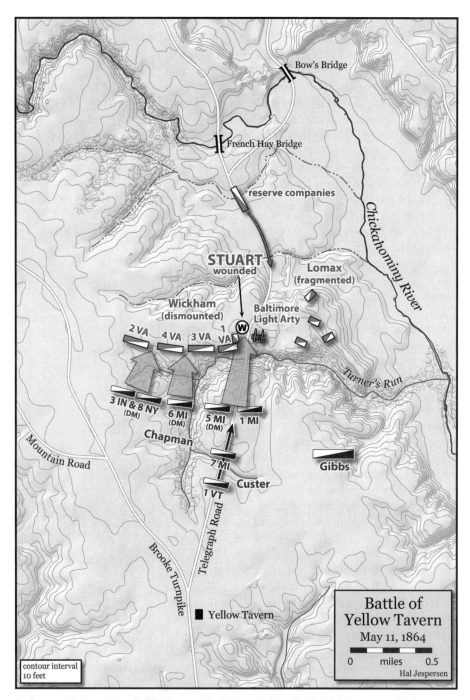

BATTLE OF YELLOW TAVERN—The bulk of the Yellow Tavern battlefield has been swallowed by development. The area of Custer's reconnaissance after the opening phase and his assault on Stuart's line is now occupied by an interstate. Visitors can still see portions of the Telegraph Road, the Stuart Monument, and the ridge occupied by the Confederates.

Light Artillery. Steadily, the Federals gained the upper hand and the Confederates began to retreat. Stuart, in an effort to rally his men, rode to the scene. He personally joined in the fight, discharging his revolver into the blue ranks.

Confederate reserves were close at hand, and elements from the 1st Virginia launched a counterattack that temporarily drove back the Wolverines. "As they retired," recalled Capt. G. W. Dorsey of the 1st Virginia, "one man who had been dismounted in the charge, and was running out on foot, turned as he passed the general, and discharging his pistol inflicted the mortal wound." Stuart reeled in the saddle, then was helped down and hastened into an ambulance that sped off for Richmond. Still, he died the following evening.

Driven back by the Confederate counterattack, the broken ranks of the 1st Michigan streamed to the rear. As had become his custom, Custer was near the front and where the fighting was the heaviest. A trooper in the 7th Michigan spotted him, "his graceful figure erect in the saddle, and his face flashing with the glow imparted by participation in the . . . charge." Undeterred by the repulse, he waved his sabre on to his remaining regiments. The added weight of the 1st Vermont and 7th Michigan prevented the Confederates from regaining a foothold on the ridge. Combined with pressure applied by Chapman's regiments, the gray positioned collapsed. "The enemy . . . fled so precipitously as to leave a large number of cartridges, carbines and equipment on the ground," a Vermonter recalled.

Custer inspected the fought-over ridge, carefully avoiding the dead and wounded. Storm clouds gathered above. It being late in the day, he directed his scattered regiments to reform. Putting spurs to his horse, he cantered back to the Union lines to select a place to bivouac. Raindrops began to fall as darkness spread across the countryside.

Trevilian Station

CHAPTER EIGHT

Shouts of men and screams of wounded horses cut through the June afternoon, only to be drowned out by gunfire. Squadrons of gray crashed into those in blue, the ranks coming so close at times that men fired into each other's faces. Despite a fiercely determined enemy, the Union troopers held their ground. At the center of the maelstrom stood Brig. Gen. George Armstrong Custer. His guidon waving overhead, Custer joined in the action, discharging his pistol at the oncoming Confederates. The intermingling ranks made their position resemble a large circle rather than a battle line. Pausing to reload, an officer approached Custer and requested to move their wagons to a place of safety. Custer assented then, as he turned to direct the movement, exclaimed, "Where in hell is the rear?!"

* * *

Following the battle at Yellow Tavern, Phil Sheridan gave his men a few hours of rest and then headed his column south along the Brook Turnpike. Skirting to the east early on the morning of May 12, Sheridan's leading division under James Wilson became entangled in the Richmond defenses, and enemy cavalry harassed the rear of the column. Threatened with being surrounded, Sheridan ordered Custer to repair Meadow Bridge over the Chickahominy, which had been destroyed by the Confederates, and open a way to safety.

Custer sent the 5th and 6th Michigan over a nearby railroad trestle to provide cover for the

Elements from Brig. Gen. Thomas L. Rosser's Laurel Brigade attacked across this field in response to the Michigan Brigade's assault on Maj. Gen. Wade Hampton's wagon train. (dd)

pioneers working on the bridge repairs. "The enemy artillery swept the bridge," wrote Major Kidd. "One man, or at most two or three, at a time, they tiptoed from tie to tie, watching the change to make it in the intervals between the shells." When they reached the opposite side, the Wolverines engaged Fitzhugh Lee's division while their comrades rebuilt the bridge. Supported by elements from Devin's brigade along with the rest of the division and after an "obstinate engagement," Custer opened the road for the Union escape. Sheridan led the corps on to Bottoms Bridge and then to Malvern Hill. The tired troopers rode into Haxall's Landing on May 14. Outnumbered and without the leadership of Stuart, the Confederates elected not to attack, giving the blue troopers a much-needed rest.

Custer took advantage of the solitude to scribble a few words to Libbie. "We have passed through days of carnage and have lost heavily. . . . The Michigan Brigade has covered itself with undying glory. . . . [W]e mortally wounded Genl. Stuart." Since the beginning of the campaign, the brigade had suffered 33 killed, 123 wounded, and 35 missing.

Following this repose, Sheridan struck out north to find the Army of the Potomac. Several days later, they trotted into Union lines above the North Anna River. Since Sheridan had left the army, Grant and Meade had engaged the Army of Northern Virginia for eleven more days around Spotsylvania. Unable to break the Confederate lines, Grant decided to turn Lee's right flank and march south toward the Virginia Central Railroad. Lee countered and

The Chickahominy River at Meadow Bridge looks more like a swamp than a river. (dd)

eventually stopped the Federals again at the North Anna, where the armies fought to a standstill.

Now Grant decided on a much larger turning movement. This time he would move southeast to the Pamunkey River. On May 26, with Sheridan's cavalry in the advance, Grant and Meade began to pull out of their position along the North Anna. Custer led the advance of the 1st Division, now back in the hands of Alfred Torbert. The Wolverines crossed the Pamunkey at Dabney's Ferry to establish a bridgehead. Throughout the next day, Custer skirmished with Confederates around Hanovertown and Crump's Creek.

Meanwhile, Lee had also abandoned his lines and marched to get between the Yankees and Richmond. Without adequate information regarding Grant's whereabouts, on the morning of May 28, Robert E. Lee dispatched the cavalry divisions of Maj. Gens. Wade Hampton, Fitzhugh Lee, and W. H. F. Lee in the direction of the Pamunkey. While Lee had not formally named a successor to Stuart, as the senior officer, Hampton held nominal command of his mounted forces.

A few miles west of Enon Church, near the settlement of Haw's Shop, Hampton encountered David Gregg's division. "The enemy dismounted, were strongly posted in a dense woods, and, in addition to defensive works, were still further

At Haw's Shop, Custer's Wolverines advanced toward this position, held by part of Col. Williams C. Wickham's brigade, from the far distance. Pressure from Custer's attack and a false report that Union infantry was moving in on the Confederate left caused the Southern line to crumble. (dd)

After the engagement at Haw's Shop, Custer established his headquarters nearby at Salem Church. (dd)

Custer and Brig. Gen. Wesley Merritt's brigade advanced across this ground during the initial phases of the fighting around the Cold Harbor crossroads on the last day of May 1864. (dd)

protected in their position by swamps," Gregg wrote. "For some hours the contest was thus maintained under a heavy and destructive fire." Toward the middle of the afternoon, Custer and the rest of the 1st Division arrived from guarding the river crossings. Custer dismounted his men, placing the 1st and 6th Michigan on his right while the 5th and 7th Michigan formed the left. He ordered an advance, and as the line approached Gregg's, the blue troopers opened a gap for the Wolverines so that they went in at a run.

"The Fifth and Seventh in their advance were exposed to a well-directed cross-fire from the enemy as well as to a heavy fire from their front," Custer remembered. In order to relieve his two regiments, Custer decided to launch a concerted assault with the 1st and 6th Michigan. He galloped to the front, removed his hat, and called for three cheers. Enthused, the Wolverines charged, their attack breaking the Confederate line. By nightfall, the Federals held the field.

On the heels of their victory at Haw's Shop, Sheridan moved his men to Old Church as the Army of the Potomac lumbered away from the Pamunkey and faced Lee along Totopotomoy Creek. Custer and his brigade encamped near New Castle Ferry before joining their comrades on May 30. Pushing south, Custer and Merritt—who was back in command of the Reserve Brigade—reinforced Devin, then engaged with Brig. Gen. Matthew C. Butler's horsemen near Matadequin Creek. Custer dismounted the 1st and 7th Michigan and placed them on the left of his line while the 5th Michigan formed the right. "I ordered them to advance," he recalled, and "the men went forward with a yell, and in a very short time we had driven the enemy from his position."

Determined to keep the pressure on the Confederates to his front, Sheridan ordered his cavalry out the following afternoon. Custer and Merritt were to resume their attack while Devin moved along an adjacent road to flank the Confederate position. After ordering the 6th Michigan to the left to link with Devin's brigade, Custer arrived at the front to find Merritt "hotly engaged . . . with . . . cavalry, infantry and artillery."

Repeated attacks failed to carry the Confederate line, and with Devin bogged down due to the heavily wooded terrain, the Federals decided on a new plan. Instead of turning the enemy's right, they would concentrate their effort on the opposite end of the line. The Reserve Brigade, supported by the 5th Michigan, managed to turn the Confederate left. As the line began to fold, Custer sent the 1st Michigan in a mounted charge that sent the gray soldiers running for the rear in confusion.

This engagement gave Sheridan possession of a crossroads known as Cold Harbor. Both Grant and Lee recognized the importance of this junction, which had roads radiating toward the Union army's supply base on the Pamunkey in one direction and the Confederate capital of Richmond in the other. Sheridan was ordered to hold it "at all hazards" until Federal infantry could arrive to secure it.

"Before the first streaks of dawn began to appear in the east" on June 1, Maj. Gen. Joseph Kershaw's Confederate division launched an assault to dislodge the blue cavalrymen. Custer sat astride his mount as the enemy advanced, directing well-placed salvos from the artillery. As the Wolverines poured a "furious" fire into the enemy ranks, he left the guns and rode along the line inspecting the action. At one point, he ordered several members of the 6th Michigan, who were laying directly in front of the cannons, to move so that they would not be injured by friendly fire.

Fortunately, Sheridan's troopers held on, and the VI Corps arrived to relieve them early in the afternoon. More Confederate infantry also reached the field, and the two armies soon faced each other on a new line for control of Cold Harbor. In one last effort to break Lee's will, Grant launched an army-wide attack two days later, but the Southerners held.

*　*　*

In nearly a month's fighting, the Union general in chief had maneuvered Lee to the doorstep of Richmond but had not dealt the devastating blow he had hoped for. Ever resilient, Grant decided to abandon Cold Harbor, cross the James River, and attempt to capture the rail junction of Petersburg. To support this movement, Grant planned to use Sheridan as a diversion. Grant ordered the

Purported to be the wealthiest man in the South in 1861, Hampton personally raised and equipped his own unit. He commanded infantry until the summer of 1862 before accepting a brigadier general's position in Stuart's cavalry, where he distinguished himself on the raid and the battlefield. His victory over Sheridan at Trevilian Station ultimately brought him command of Stuart's old corps. (loc)

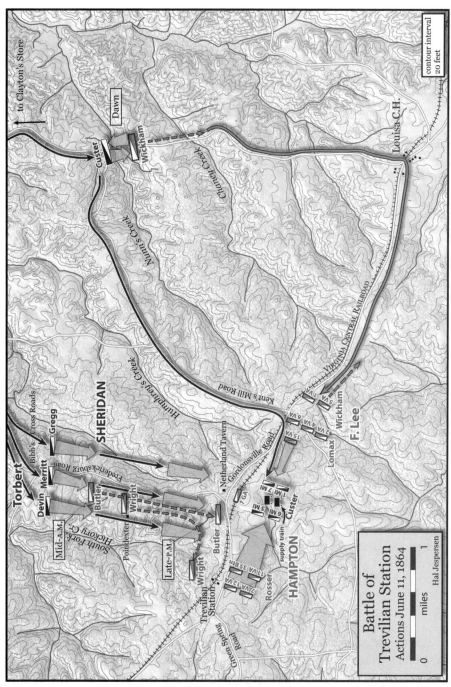

BATTLE OF TREVILIAN STATION—Leaving his encampment early on the morning of June 11, Custer led his brigade toward Trevilian Station along the Nunn's Creek Road to the Kent's Mill Road and finally to the Gordonsville Road before he discovered Hampton's wagon train. The area of Custer's fight is now private property. The site of Hampton's wagon park is a modern lumberyard.

cavalry commander to march west, break up the Virginia Central Railroad, and then move on to the Shenandoah Valley to make contact with Union forces under Maj. Gen. David Hunter. Sheridan chose Gregg and Torbert for the expedition, and the divisions rendezvoused at New Castle Ferry.

While rations and ammunition were issued to the troopers, Custer took a few moments to write Libbie:

The Michigan Cavalry Brigade camped in this field on the night of June 10. (dd)

To-morrow morning two Divisions . . . of this Corps set out on another raid. We may be gone two or three weeks. I will write, the first opportunity. Keep up a stout heart . . . God and success have hitherto attended us. May we not hope for a continuance of His blessing? With thoughts of my darling and with the holy inspiration of a just and noble cause, I gladly set out to discharge my duty to my country with a willing heart. Need I repeat to my darling that while living she is my all, and if Destiny wills me to die, wills that my country needs my death, my last prayer will be for her, my last breath will speak her name and that Heaven will not be Heaven till we are joined together.

The Union horsemen crossed the Pamunkey and struck out to the northeast. Three days of hard marching brought Custer to a point three miles north of Louisa Court House. Torbert and Gregg bivouacked a few miles behind Custer. Sheridan planned an advance the next morning on Trevilian Station, a stop on the Virginia Central, where he expected to meet the Confederates. Sheridan directed Custer to turn the enemy flank and capture the station.

Confederate cavalry had reacted swiftly to Sheridan's march. Wade Hampton and Fitzhugh Lee had departed with the Army of Northern Virginia a day after the Federal expedition. "Supposing he would strike at Gordonsville and Charlottesville, I moved rapidly . . . to interpose my command . . . in two days' march I accomplished my objective," Hampton wrote. As Sheridan bedded down on the night of June 10, Hampton was only a few miles away and Lee's division was at Louisa, directly facing Custer.

This Civil War Trails marker stands north of Louisa Court House and details the early morning skirmish between Custer's brigade and Fitzhugh Lee's division. (dd)

Netherland Tavern served as Hampton's headquarters prior to the battle. Nearby, a section of James Thomson's Ashby Horse Artillery engaged Custer to the south. Maj. James Hart's Washington (South Carolina) Artillery joined Thomas later in the fight. A reconstructed tavern now stands near the structure's original site. (dd)

Around 3:30 a.m. on June 11, Brig. Gen. Williams Wickham's brigade struck pickets from the 7th Michigan. Roused from his slumber, Custer sent the 1st Michigan to reinforce their comrades, and Wickham was driven back to the Confederate camps. Custer did not seem to be bothered by this skirmish and, after sunrise, mounted his command and headed out.

Moving along a wooded road, the sound of gunfire from the west soon reached the ears of Custer's troopers as Hampton engaged Torbert and Gregg. Suddenly, a rider approached with the news that a large enemy wagon train had been spotted around Trevilian Station. This discovery meant that Custer was close to the enemy's rear. If he could seize the wagons, it would not only cripple the enemy's supplies but offer the possibility of trapping Hampton between the Michigan brigade and Sheridan. Custer immediately ordered Col. Russell Alger and the 5th Michigan ahead. "This regiment charged . . . capturing a large number of wagons, ambulances, caissons, and . . . led horses," he recalled. Custer then sent the 6th Michigan forward in support. Riding to the aid of the 5th Michigan, the 6th Michigan came under fire from a detachment of Confederate troopers.

Custer soon galloped into the station, dismounted, and ordered Pennington to unlimber and prepare to fight. Driving back the enemy cavalry who had surprised the 6th Michigan, he directed the 7th Michigan to the field as troopers from Hampton's division began to materialize from the woods to the north. Apprised of Custer's movement, Hampton pulled back to deal with this threat. Brigadier General Thomas Rosser's brigade struck the Wolverines near the station. Rosser's attack prompted Custer to send a man back to bring up the 1st Michigan, only to find this regiment was also embroiled in the fight.

Unknowingly, Custer had advanced through a gap between the two Confederate divisions. Fitzhugh Lee had marched to the sound of the firing from Louisa and had struck the rear of Custer's brigade, driving the 1st Michigan back toward the station. This assault gobbled up Custer's own wagons. "Would you like to know what they have captured from me?" he wrote Libbie several days later. "Everything except my toothbrush. They only captured one wagon from me, but that contained my all—bedding, desk, sword-belt, underclothing, and my commission as General which arrived a few days before."

Custer was now caught in a vice between Hampton and Lee, his brigade surrounded. The men were "engaged in three different directions at once," recalled an officer in the 7th Michigan. Any hope of survival would depend upon Custer holding on until the rest of the command came to his rescue. Never had their Spencer repeaters been put to more important use. Under Custer's eye, the Wolverines stood firm, his personal actions a source of inspiration.

Early on the morning of June 12, Custer established his headquarters here at Charles Goodall Trevilian's house. Mr. Trevilian's daughter was sick with typhoid fever inside. Before departing, Custer directed his surgeon to leave medicine behind for the family. (kb-d)

In the aftermath of one assault, a wounded man from the 5th Michigan "fell in a position as still exposed to enemy fire." Catching sight of him, Custer rushed forward, picked him up, and carried him to safety. When Pennington reported the loss of one of his cannons, Custer organized a small detachment and led them in a charge that recaptured it. Striking it with his sabre he exclaimed to Pennington, "there is your gun; take it." Then turning to the Confederates, he yelled, "I am General Custer. If you want this piece, come and take it." During one attack, his personal color bearer, Sgt. Mitchell Beloir of the 1st Michigan, was killed. Custer ripped the guidon from its standard and stuffed it inside his uniform coat to keep it from being captured.

After several hours of fighting, Merritt was able to break through and relieve the beleaguered Wolverines. With the Federal command united, Hampton decided to break off the fight and withdraw to the west. His brigade secure, Custer led the 7th Michigan in pursuit of Lee and managed to recapture several of his own brigade's wagons. With the Confederates gone from their front, Sheridan set up camp around the station.

The following afternoon, Sheridan directed Gregg to destroy the railroad running east to Louisa while Torbert led a reconnaissance to the west. Despite their rough handling the day before, Custer led the advance. "We had marched but a few miles when we found the enemy in a very strong position," he wrote. Custer dismounted the 6th and 7th Michigan and sent them forward to probe Hampton's line. When the regiments became "hotly engaged," Merritt came up and deployed on the Michigan brigade's right. Custer added the 1st and 5th Michigan to the line, and the "engagement

Following the engagement on June 11, Hampton withdrew to the west and formed a new line around the Ogg Farm. (dd)

became general." As the remainder of Torbert's division joined in the action, Torbert ordered Custer to advance and "dislodge the enemy." Custer, however, now held back. He was in a relative state of shock, haunted by the previous day's events. His ranks had been depleted, having lost 25 killed, 82 wounded, and 309 missing. Additionally, Custer recognized the strength of the enemy's position. Rather than risk an all-out assault, he was content to allow his men to engage Hampton at long range and keep the Confederates on that end of the line in check from reinforcing against Merritt.

The Michigan Brigade moved against Hampton's position on the Ogg Farm from the left of the photograph. (dd)

Early in the evening, Hampton directed Lee to launch a flank attack. Supported by a battery, Lee sent Lunsford Lomax's brigade crashing into the Union line, which forced Torbert back to Trevilian Station.

This setback convinced Sheridan of the futility of additional fighting. Hampton had brought Sheridan's movement across Virginia to a grinding halt, and the Union cavalry commander decided to abandon the expedition. So as not to alert the enemy of his withdrawal, Sheridan decided to move out under cover of darkness on June 13.

The last flickering rays of sunlight danced through the trees as the Michigan brigade shuffled into column and prepared to march. Custer's thoughts, however, remained with the unburied bodies of the men he had led for almost a year. Never had they "fought so long or so desperately," he remembered. A somberness came over him. He very well knew that it could have been him lying there, too. During the fight, he had been struck several times, but fortunately the bullets were spent. With a heavy heart, he took his place once again at the head of his troopers.

In the Shenandoah Valley

CHAPTER NINE

Autumn leaves were still changing colors, but the smell of snow was in the air. A small group of horsemen trotted along a dirt road, here and there passing a cavalryman on the ground. Some were wounded; others didn't move. Suddenly, without any warning, the officer in front turned and galloped off to the left. Reaching a high ridge, George Armstrong Custer came in full view of a Confederate battle line. It stood just across a stream that ran below him and on top of a hill directly to his front. He scanned the position until his eyes caught sight of a familiar figure. Custer spurred onward along the crest so that he could be plainly seen by men on both sides. Removing his hat, in one grand motion, he swept it from his left shoulder across his body and bowed.

* * *

"June was consumed in the return march to the army," Maj. James Kidd remembered after Trevilian Station. By the end of the month, they reached the Union lines opposite Petersburg and bivouacked near Reams's Station. "Men and horses are worn out from marches and the absence of food," Custer informed Libbie. Two days later, they returned to the James and encamped at Light House Point.

After nearly two months of campaigning, the Wolverines could enjoy a brief rest. The ranks

A small stream, Tom's Brook, served as a barrier between Rosser and Custer on October 9, 1864. (dd)

This photograph of Custer was taken in July, 1864, shortly after his return from the Trevilian Raid. (loc)

swelled as convalescents and wounded rejoined the command. "Many also who had been dismounted by the exigencies of the campaign returned from dismounted camps," Kidd wrote. "A fine lot of new horses were received. During the month the condition of the animals were very much improved, good care and a plentiful supply of forage contributing to the result."

Still, Custer was plagued by his experience and brush with death at Trevilian Station. "I frequently discover myself acting as umpire between my patriotism and my desire to be and remain with my darling," he wrote Libbie on July 1. "I do not enter the Army, as some do leaving wealth, position, a comfortable home—but I do infinitely more, I separate myself from my heart's darling. But it will not always be so. A better time is in store for us."

Fortunately, he received some relief during a visit from Libbie. In the company of several congressmen and senators, she traveled from Washington to City Point. "Autie, on watch for the steamer, chartered a small boat, too impatient to wait. As he approached our anchored ship, standing in the small boat, shouted, and waving his hat, the party cheered . . . as soon as he leaped on deck, lifting me in the air, and overwhelming me with demonstrations of affection. Then . . . he dropped me . . . as it were and shook everybody's hand, talking vehemently, words tumbling over one another."

The couple was able to enjoy a few days of solitude, but events elsewhere in Virginia would soon pull Custer back into the field. While Grant moved on Petersburg, Robert E. Lee had detached his Second Corps under Lt. Gen. Jubal Early west to the Shenandoah Valley. Early's task was to contend with Maj. Gen. David Hunter's Federal army advancing on the logistical center of Lynchburg. Lee also hoped this movement would force Grant to deplete his own numbers and send reinforcements to the Valley. Arriving in the middle of June, Early trounced Hunter, then marched north down the Valley to enter Maryland. Defeating a Federal force at Monocacy, his force approached the outer defenses of Washington. Rather than hazard an attack, he skirmished with elements of the VI Corps sent by Grant to reinforce the city. Early then withdrew into Virginia. The Confederates' audacity convinced Union leadership that a new commander was necessary to deal with Early's force. Grant chose Philip Sheridan for the assignment.

At the end of July, Custer and the 1st Cavalry Division left their position near Prince George Court House below Petersburg and marched to City Point for transport to Washington. From there they travelled overland to Harper's Ferry to rendezvous with Sheridan's new Army of the Shenandoah. This force consisted of the VI Corps and the XVIV Corps, fresh from Louisiana, along with two divisions commanded by Maj. Gen. George Crook. Sheridan appointed Alfred Torbert to lead his mounted forces, which consisted of Torbert's 1st Division and another commanded by Brig. Gen. William W. Averell. Brigadier General James Wilson's division, en route from the Army of the Potomac, would augment this corps of cavalry. Wesley Merritt once again assumed command of Torbert's division while Torbert took on his larger responsibilities.

Known as Robert E. Lee's "Bad Old Man," Jubal Early's operations in the Shenandoah Valley and Maryland during the summer of 1864 caused tremendous consternation among the Union high command. (loc)

"In pushing up the Shenandoah Valley . . . it is desirable that nothing should be left to invite the enemy to return," Grant directed Sheridan. "Take all provisions, forage and stock wanted for the use of your command. Such as cannot be consumed, destroy. . . . [T]he object is to drive the enemy south. . . . [B]e guided in your course by the course he takes."

Sheridan's movement got under way during the second week of August. Torbert's cavalry, with Merritt as the vanguard, headed south toward Berryville. Sheridan's infantry followed, with the hope of flanking Early at Bunker Hill. Custer led the advance toward Winchester the following morning, the division skirmishing with enemy cavalry along the way before turning toward Newtown. Sheridan's movement proved successful as Early marched south and assumed a new position at Fisher's Hill, some three miles below Strasburg. Sheridan followed, but decided not to test the strength of Early's line.

While the two armies glared at each other, Merritt moved toward Front Royal. Around mid-day on August 16, Maj. Gen. Fitzhugh Lee's division, which had forded the Shenandoah River, surprised Custer's brigade. Pickets from the 6th Michigan managed to hold Lee off long enough for

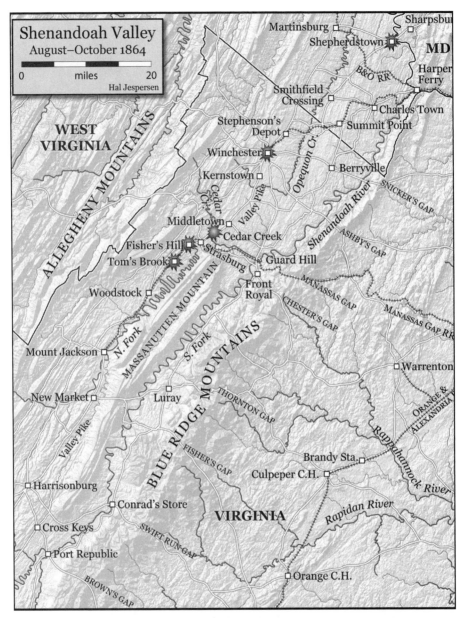

SHENANDOAH VALLEY—Sheridan's theater of operations stretched from Winchester in a southwesterly direction to Harrisonburg, with a number of towns and villages in between. A macadamized highway, known as the Valley Turnpike, served as the main thoroughfare. The region was bounded on the west by the Alleghenies and on the east by a long range known as Massanutten. East of Massanutten stretched the Luray Valley, which was bordered on the east by the Blue Ridge Mountains. A number of streams ran through the region along with the two forks of the Shenandoah River.

Custer to send the 5th Michigan to their support. Accompanied by his staff, Custer rode to an eminence overlooking the ford to find Confederate infantry attempting to cross in support of the cavalry. Custer deployed his troopers "into line in fine style and opened . . . a hot fire." Elements from Col. Thomas Devin's brigade soon arrived to reinforce the Wolverines. Together, Custer and Devin directed their troopers and successfully pushed back the combined enemy force.

At Kearneysville, Custer moved his brigade and the 1st New York Dragoons across this ground in an effort to extricate them in the face of superior Confederate numbers. (dd)

The infantry Custer and Devin had encountered turned out to be part of Lt. Gen. Richard Anderson's First Corps, sent by Robert E. Lee to reinforce Early. Anderson's movement into the Luray Valley posed the risk of turning Sheridan's left, so the Union commander decided to withdraw.

Merritt's division marched to Berryville. After several days in the vicinity, they moved on to Shepherdstown. Sheridan and the infantry established a new line around Halltown, the Confederates close on their heels. On August 25th, Merritt and Wilson launched a reconnaissance in the direction of Leetown but ran into Lt. Gen. John C. Breckenridge's Confederate corps. A sharp fight ensued, and when the Confederates brought up reinforcements, Torbert decided to disengage and fall back.

Custer led his men toward the Potomac. The sound of gunfire to his front attracted his attention. Accompanied by his staff, he spurred ahead. The small party soon encountered Confederate cavalry. Slashing through, Custer made his way over a high rise and ran into the 1st New York Dragoons, who had been detailed as Merritt's rear guard. Custer directed the Empire Staters to charge the Southerners. The ensuing attack opened a gap for the Wolverines to unite with their comrades, and the march continued.

After Kearneysville, Custer crossed the Potomac River at Boteler's Ford and reached the safety of the north bank. (dd)

Nearing the river, he ordered a dismount to give his men a breather. This brief rest ended when gray cavalry appeared to their front and Breckenridge's infantry emerged at their rear. "In a few moments, the enemy's right and left flanks began to swing in toward the river," Major Kidd wrote, threatening to cut off Custer's line of retreat to the Potomac. "With surprising coolness," Custer calmly deployed

Custer's brigade forced a crossing at Locke's Ford on Opequon Creek in the opening stages of the battle of Third Winchester. (dd)

his regiments. From right to left, he placed the 6th Michigan, 1st Michigan, 5th Michigan, and 7th Michigan. The Confederate infantry slowly probed the line, forming a "horseshoe" around the blue troopers.

"There was not a hint of weakness or fear in any quarter," Kidd proudly recalled. Custer directed his men to fall back, deploying into column and then into a line of battle, "as if on parade" as they slowly made their way to the river. Somehow, he was able to find a ford, and the regiments crossed one at a time into Maryland and safety. Similar to Amissville, Custer had once again been able to safely withdraw his men in the face of a larger Confederate force.

By early September, Sheridan had moved up about 25 miles and occupied a line in Virginia around Clifton and Berryville. In the middle of the month, he learned Anderson had been called back to Petersburg. Stirred to action, he decided to attack Early outside Winchester. His plan called for the infantry to advance along the Berryville Turnpike and strike the Confederates east of town. The bulk of Torbert's horsemen, including Merritt's division and Custer's brigade, drew the assignment of securing the upper fords of Opequon Creek and covering the army's right.

About 2 a.m. on September 19, Custer shook his brigade out of their camps around Summit Point and, with the rest of Merritt's division, made their way toward the Opequon. Arriving atop a ridge overlooking Locke's Ford, Custer prepared to force his away across. The 25th New York Cavalry, assigned to the brigade due to the losses sustained in the spring campaigns, was to lead the way, supported by the 7th Michigan. Opposing them were Breckinridge's Confederates. When the Federals "reached the water . . . the enemy from a well-covered rifle pit opposite the crossing, opened a heavy fire upon our advance and succeeded in repulsing the head of the column," Custer wrote. Relentless, Custer ordered the 6th Michigan to lay down a covering as the 1st Michigan charged across the ford. This second effort succeeded, and Custer established a bridgehead on the south bank.

The Confederates fell back and reformed. Cooperating with Col. Charles R. Lowell's brigade,

Custer once again sent the 25th New York and 7th Michigan forward to test this new position. Although it initially proved too strong, the gray-clad soldiers eventually withdrew. While Sheridan and Early battled in the fields around Winchester, Custer ordered his troopers into column and headed west with the rest of the division. Reaching the vicinity of the Martinsburg Pike, he made contact with Averell. With the two divisions united, Merritt and Averell deployed into line of battle and advanced south to the sound of the guns.

"Most, if not all of the brigades moved by brigade front, regiments being in parallel columns or squadrons," Custer wrote.

One continuous and heavy fire of skirmishers covered the advance, using only the carbine, while the line of brigades as they advanced across the open country, the bands playing the national airs, presented in the sunlight one moving mass of glittering sabers. This, combined with the various and bright-colored banners and battle-flags, intermingled here and there with the plain blue uniforms of the troops, furnished

Fort Collier was squarely in the path of the massive Union cavalry charge at Third Winchester. (kb-d)

Alfred Torbert failed to trap Early's army during the engagement at Fisher's Hill, and Sheridan never forgave him for the misstep. When Torbert went home on leave several months later, Sheridan never recalled him to command. (loc)

Custer succeeded James H. Wilson in command of the 3rd Cavalry Division. Wilson went on to great success commanding cavalry in the Western Theater and played a pivotal role at the battle of Nashville. After his discharge in 1870, he engaged in a number of business ventures until the Spanish-American War, when he was commissioned a major general of volunteers. He served in Cuba and Puerto Rico and participated in the Boxer Rebellion in 1901. (loc)

one of the most inspiring as well as imposing scenes of martial grandeur ever witnessed upon a battle-field.

The Union cavalry slammed into the divisions of Maj. Gens. Lunsford Lomax and Fitzhugh Lee, pushing them back upon Early's left flank. In conjunction with this assault, Sheridan pressed his infantry forward upon the enemy center. This pressure up and down the line forced the Confederates to break. As the line gave way, Merritt ordered Custer to launch one more attack. Forming into a single line, Custer ordered his bugler to sound the charge. "The enemy upon our approach turned and delivered a well-directed volley of musketry but before a second discharge could be given my command was in their midst, sabering right and left," he recalled. "Further resistance on the part of those opposed to us was suspended." Early's army collapsed, and the retreat escalated into a rout. His men scampered through town, heading south along the Valley Pike.

Custer had little time to rest. Merritt's division set out after Early the following morning. Riding through Strasburg, some 20 miles away, they once again found the Confederates, now ensconced atop Fisher's Hill. This time, Sheridan decided to attack. Part of his plan called for Torbert to proceed up the Luray Valley, through the Massanutten passes, and cut off the enemy's line of retreat. The Federals got underway on the morning of September 21 and headed south to Milford. There they encountered enemy cavalry in a strong position and, rather than risk an assault, returned to Front Royal to spend the night. The next day Merritt marched back to Milford and found the Confederate line abandoned. Custer and Lowell set out for Luray the following morning. Three miles north of the village, the Federals encountered and "whipped" Williams Wickham's brigade in an engagement that could hardly be considered a skirmish. Custer then led his men through Luray Gap to New Market and south to Harrisonburg.

Unfortunately, Torbert was late. Although Union infantry had successfully stormed Fisher's Hill and again defeated the Confederates, Early had been able to move fast enough to escape the closing vice. His demoralized army marched south and eventually vacated the Valley. The Federal cavalry's inability to deal a decisive blow to the enemy infuriated Sheridan. He directed his anger toward William Averell, who, he believed, had failed to launch an aggressive pursuit after the battle. He promptly relieved Averell and replaced him with Custer. However, Custer held this new post for only several days. At the end of the month, as the army enjoyed a brief respite around Harrisonburg, James Wilson received orders assigning him as Chief of Cavalry for Maj. Gen. William T. Sherman's armies in the west. In turn, Sheridan chose Custer to lead the 3rd Cavalry Division. "Am I not fortunate?" a pleased Custer wrote to Libbie.

Promoted to brigadier general the same day as Custer in June 1863, Wesley Merritt commanded the Reserve Brigade and later the 1st Cavalry Division. One of the most accomplished cavalryman of the war, Merritt later commanded the 5th United States and 9th United States Cavalry during the Indian Wars. He led the Manila Expedition in the Spanish American War. (loc)

This new command consisted of two brigades led by Col. Alexander Pennington, the reliable artillerist once attached to the Michigan Brigade, and Col. William Wells. "The Div[sic] feel very much pleased with the change," Wells wrote in a letter home. "We have a gallant leader." A trooper in the 8th New York Cavalry echoed this sentiment. "The boys liked General Custer," he recalled. "There was some get up and get to him. He used the saber a great deal which the boys . . . liked. They were at home with the saber."

Sheridan spent the next several days destroying anything of military value in the area. At the end of the first week of October, the Army of the Shenandoah struck out for Winchester. Torbert's horsemen brought up the army's rear where the devastation of the countryside continued. Custer marched along the Back Road while Merritt covered the Valley Turnpike. In the midst of the withdrawal, Confederate cavalry appeared. Reinforced, Early had decided to follow Sheridan at a distance.

As Lunsford Lomax nipped at Merritt's heels, Custer had to endure harassment from the division of Maj. Gen. Thomas L. Rosser. The two knew each other very well, having been acquaintances at West Point before the war. Rosser had begun the conflict as an artillerist before he transferred to the mounted arm to lead the 5th Virginia Cavalry. Like his foe, Rosser had risen to command through his skill and bravery in battle. He had been wounded at First Manassas,

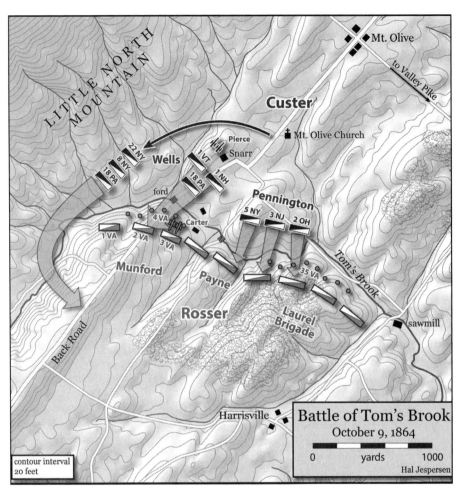

Battle of Tom's Brook
October 9, 1864

contour interval
20 feet

0   yards   1000
Hal Jespersen

BATTLE OF TOM'S BROOK—In the initial stages of the battle, Custer probed Rosser's front. When he found it too strong, he promptly sent a flanking force around the Confederate left, which proved successful.

Mechanicsville, and more recently at Trevilian Station while engaged with Custer's Wolverines.

Rosser's and Lomax's action also attracted the attention of Phil Sheridan. Disgusted that his cavalry had not simply turned and brushed aside the pesky Confederates, he directed Torbert on the evening of October 8 to "Go out there in the morning and whip that Rebel cavalry or get whipped yourself." Orders went out to Custer and Merritt to launch an attack the next morning. Shortly before 6 a.m., Custer's division stirred from its camp on the Back Road. Pennington's brigade led the advance as Custer trotted south.

Around Mount Olive Church, the Federals encountered Confederate skirmishers. Not expecting to face an entire brigade, the gray cavalryman gave ground, falling back to their main line on high ground overlooking a stream known as Tom's Brook. Custer rode with his staff near the head of Pennington's column before leaving them to observe the enemy for himself. Custer saw Rosser's division stretched before him. Rosser had placed Col. Thomas Munford's brigade on the left, with Munford's right resting on the Back Road. On Munford's right and in the center stood Col. William Payne's brigade and beyond them, Col. Richard Dulany's veteran Laurel Brigade. Custer recognized his old friend and extended a cordial salute.

At first glance, Rosser's line appeared strong, yet Custer elected to probe it. Keeping Wells in reserve and under cover, he ordered Pennington to send forward a mounted attack, which consisted of the 5th New York, 2nd Ohio, and 3rd New Jersey. Captain Charles Pierce's combined Batteries B and L, 2nd United States Artillery lent their support to Pennington. Despite Pierce's guns firing with "spirit," Pennington met stiff resistance from Munford and Payne. His troopers managed to reach the north bank of Tom's Brook before they were driven back.

After the war, Tom Rosser became the chief engineer of the Northern Pacific and Canadian Pacific Railroads. He was also a staunch supporter of his former friend and foe, Custer. (gig)

From Custer's view, another head-on assault was fruitless. Peering off to his left, the right of Rosser's position seemed formidable. He concluded that the left flank must be the weak point and prepared to assail the enemy again. This time, the main effort would be in the form of a turning column. The 8th New York, 22nd New York, and 18th Pennsylvania drew this assignment. While these regiments attempted to locate the enemy's left, Wells would add his weight to Pennington's line in the hopes of keeping Rosser's attention occupied on his front.

Preparations complete, Custer ordered a renewal of the assault. Typical of his conduct in battle, although uncommon for a division commander, he dismounted and personally led the 5th New York forward. "Soon the whole line was in motion," wrote an officer in the 18th Pennsylvania, "and advanced as rapidly as the nature of the ground and wearied condition of my horses would allow, driving the enemy's skirmishers before it." Although receiving a heavy fire, the New Yorkers and Pennsylvanians "did not waver" and slammed into Munford's troopers.

Skirmishers from the 5th New York Cavalry encountered the 4th Virginia Cavalry here at Mt. Olive and opened the battle on Custer's front. (dd)

This pressure, combined with that to his front, caused Rosser's line to crumble.

Rosser retreated for about two miles before he reformed and launched a counterattack, which was turned back with the help of Pierce's artillery. Wells and Pennington quickly deployed, and "the whole line moved forward at the charge," Custer wrote. "Before this irresistible advance the enemy found it impossible to stand." Once again, the Confederates collapsed, the Federals galloping after them in hot pursuit. Along the Valley Turnpike, Merritt had also routed Lomax, sending him scampering nearly 20 miles to New Market.

The day's outcome elated Custer. "Never since the opening of this war had there been witnessed such a complete and decisive overthrow of the enemy's cavalry," he remembered. Personally, it was much more—a "glorious day," as he described it to Libbie. After fifteen months leading a brigade, Sheridan had seen fit to elevate him to command a division. With additional responsibilities, his first engagement could have very well been a disaster. Instead, his bravery, poise, and decisiveness contributed to the growing number of Union victories in the Shenandoah.

The next morning, Custer celebrated. After losing his own wagon train at Buckland Mills and Trevilian Station, fittingly, he had captured Rosser's during the pursuit. Much to the delight of his men, Custer walked through their camps and greeted them in the Virginian's uniform coat.

Elements from the 1st New Hampshire Cavalry advanced from this crest against Rosser's line on the opposite ridge. Tom's Brook runs inside the treeline at the center of the picture. (dd)

Appomattox

CHAPTER TEN

Union cavalrymen dismounted among the houses and stores of the hamlet. Small parties fanned out to gather what supplies they could from the countryside while their comrades bedded down under large trees surrounded by evergreen hedges. Soon the foragers returned, and the troopers enjoyed their supper. Picket lines established, the horse soldiers drifted off for a few hours' rest.

High-pitched notes of the bugle woke them well before daylight, and by seven they were in the saddle. As the day wore on, the advance guard began to encounter Confederate soldiers. These stragglers were more interested in giving themselves up than in fighting. One of them talked too much. The information he shared startled his captors, who sent him to the division commander immediately. Escorted to the head of the column, the cooperative Rebel was soon face to face with Bvt. Maj. Gen. George Armstrong Custer.

* * *

Upon learning of the presence of Confederate supply trains at Appomattox Station on April 8, Custer dispatched Col. Alanson Randol's 2nd New York Cavalry ahead of his division to capture them. "Go in old fellow and don't let anything stop you," he told his subordinate. Randol's attack proved successful. (dd)

Following the engagement at Tom's Brook, the victorious 3rd Cavalry Division continued its march north. Custer assumed a position with the rest of the army below Middletown along Cedar Creek. Then, on October 19, in an effort to recapture his fortunes, Early attacked. When the Confederate infantry rolled up the Union left flank, Alfred Torbert summoned Custer to bolster

Sheridan established his headquarters here at Belle Grove Plantation outside Middletown. Maj. Gen. Stephen D. Ramseur, a Confederate officer and former West Point classmate of Custer's, was brought here after being mortally wounded at Cedar Creek. Custer spent much of the night at Ramseur's side before Ramseur succumbed the next morning. (dd)

the infantry line. At first driven from the field, the Federals managed to rally late in the morning. Soon after, Sheridan, who had been absent, returned from Washington, reaching the scene after riding thirteen miles from Winchester. His arrival lifted the Army of the Shenandoah's spirit.

"Looks as though we are gone up to-day," Custer said as he greeted his chief.

"The right will prevail," Sheridan forcefully replied.

"We will go back to our old camps tonight or I will sacrifice every man in my division and I will go with them," Custer vowed in return.

His division placed on the right of the line, Custer prepared to join in the counterattack. As the Union infantry moved forward, Colonel Pennington was able to occupy a low ridge that afforded Custer a view of the developing engagement. Custer noticed that the Confederate left was vulnerable. Ordering Pennington to press forward and protect his own right, Custer prepared to charge. He gave the order just as the Confederates gave way under the pressure of the infantry advance. "The effect of our movement, although differing from what we anticipated, was instantaneous and decisive," wrote Custer. "Seeing so large a force of cavalry bearing rapidly down upon an unprotected flank and their line of retreat in danger of being intercepted, the . . . enemy . . . now gave way in utmost confusion."

Early's men stampeded from the field in a race for safety. "It was no longer a question to be decided by force of arms, by skill or by courage; it was simply a question of speed between pursuers and pursued," Custer remembered.

By nightfall, Sheridan had reoccupied his camps. The battle of Cedar Creek broke the back of Early's army and left the Federals in firm control of the Shenandoah Valley.

In recognition of Custer's service during the campaign, Sheridan dispatched him to Washington to present captured enemy battle flags to Secretary of War Edwin Stanton. With Libbie in attendance at the ceremony in the Secretary's office, Stanton announced that Custer had been promoted to brevet major general. Although the promotion carried an honorary rank and not a permanent one, this unexpected revelation left Custer speechless. The near destruction of his command at Trevilian Station had hung like a pall over him since June. Through his actions at Shepherdstown, Winchester, Tom's Brook, and Cedar Creek, he'd found redemption.

Custer returned to the Valley. Libbie joined him, and the two prepared to spend the winter months together with the army around Winchester. Less than a week before Christmas, though, Custer's division was ordered south in support of an expedition against the Orange and Alexandria Railroad.

Outside Harrisonburg near the hamlet of Lacy's Springs, Custer's command was surprised in an early morning attack by Rosser's division. The Confederates broke through the Union picket

Custer presented enemy flags captured at Cedar Creek to Secretary of War Edwin Stanton. (loc)

line, but the blue cavalrymen managed to rally. Custer, who had been asleep in his headquarters at a nearby inn, rushed outside without coat or boots. "General Custer was up at full speed on a bareback steed, calling for the Second Ohio," remembered one of the troopers. "Charge to the pike! They're coming that way," he ordered. The ensuing counterattack shifted the momentum back to the Federals. Breaking off the raid, Custer returned to Winchester.

In the middle of January 1865, he managed to procure a furlough and, with Libbie, traveled back to Michigan. The experience of war had taken a toll on Custer. No longer did he yearn for a battle every day as he had expressed in a letter to his cousin in the autumn of 1862. Horrors encountered on so many fields plus the experiences at Buckland Mills and Trevilian Station had altered his perspective on life. He realized a greater power had sustained him. "Reflection . . . had convinced me that I was not fulfilling the end of my Creator if I lived for this world alone," he recalled. One night while attending prayer services at the Monroe Presbyterian Church, Custer accepted Christ as His Lord and Savior.

His furlough over, the Custers returned to Virginia just in time for the campaign season to begin. At Petersburg, Grant envisioned a new assignment for Sheridan and his cavalry. He ordered his subordinate to destroy the Virginia Central Railroad and Lynchburg, then proceed to join Union forces in North Carolina. "The hilltops of the Blue Ridge and the North Mountains were white with snow" as the blue horsemen snaked out of Winchester on February 27.

Thomas C. Devin was a house painter before the war. Commissioned colonel of the 6th New York Cavalry in November 1861, Devin eventually rose to brigade command and distinguished himself during the Gettysburg and Overland campaigns. Finally appointed to division command in early 1865, Devin was one of the most successful amateur soldiers of the war. (loc)

Despite poor weather, the column made it to Woodstock by nightfall. Custer's division had the advance when it struck out again the next morning, followed by Brig. Gen. Thomas Devin's 1st Division. With Alfred Torbert on a leave of absence, Wesley Merritt had overall command of the two divisions. The Federals continued on to Mount Crawford and then Staunton, nearly 100 miles, which they reached on March 2. There, Sheridan learned that Early and the remnants of his command had moved east to the village of Waynesboro. Sheridan immediately ordered

Custer out in pursuit. About 2 p.m., he reigned up in front of Early's line.

Custer sent Wells's brigade forward to test the position and found a gap between the Confederate left and a bend in the nearby South River. Custer decided to employ tactics similar to those he had used against Rosser at Tom's Brook. Wells, supported by Col. Henry Capehart's brigade, which had recently joined the division, would attack Early's center. Meanwhile, three regiments from Pennington's brigade, the 1st Connecticut, 2nd Ohio, and 3rd New Jersey, would work their way through the opening on the enemy flank. At Custer's signal, the assault began. "We fired as we ran, until half-way up the side of the ridge, which was so steep we were compelled to halt and rest after our run through the mud," remembered a soldier in the 2nd Ohio. "The enemy was loath to leave . . . protected by boulders and trees. . . . [W]e sprang to our feet, and their line gave way in front of us." Under pressure from front and flank, Early's line disintegrated. The chase continued to Rockfish Gap, over a half dozen miles away, with Early himself barely escaping the grasp of Custer's victorious troopers.

Sheridan's movement brought him well east of Grant's prescribed route to Lynchburg. Instead of resuming this course, he decided to carry out the instructions of destroying the Virginia Central,

Custer's division attacked the Confederate line at Five Forks from the far distance. At one point during the assault, a Confederate volley felled his bugler, color bearer, and orderly. Unscathed, Custer grabbed his guidon, waved it over his head, and led his troopers over the enemy works. (dd)

A reproduction of Custer's personal guidon that he carried throughout his military career, from the author's private collection. A variation of this guidon is on display at the Monroe County Historical Museum, in Monroe, Michigan, Custer's adopted hometown. (dd)

then rejoin his commander at Petersburg. The day after his victory at Waynesboro, Custer approached Charlottesville. On the outskirts, he was met by a delegation of citizens and the mayor, who promptly surrendered and presented him with the keys to the city and the University of Virginia. The cavalry then pressed on through Columbia, Ashland, and Hanover Junction. After reaching White House Landing on March 18, the tired troopers resupplied and rested after their journey. Moving again on the morning of March 25, the Federals crossed the James River and went into camp behind the Union lines at Petersburg.

*   *   *

Since the previous summer, Grant had maintained a steady stranglehold on the cities of Richmond and Petersburg. Only one of Robert E. Lee's supply routes remained open, the Southside Railroad. With the addition of Sheridan's force, the general in chief now planned for a final offensive. Grant instructed Sheridan to swing west toward Dinwiddie Court House and entice Lee to send infantry out of the fortifications to where it could be engaged in open country and against superior numbers. If the ploy didn't work, Sheridan was to move on and destroy the railroad.

The Union cavalry got under way on the morning of March 29. Custer and the 3rd Cavalry Division drew the assignment of guarding the wagon train and bringing up the rear of the column. "Continuous rain had made the roads almost impassable," remembered a soldier in the 1st Vermont. "We lifted and tugged at the wagons, cut trees and piled rails into the road for corduroy."

"Last night I slept on the ground by the roadside," Custer wrote to Libbie on the second day of their march. "My only protection was the fine rubber poncho. . . . [F]or pillow I had a stick laid across two parallel rails. Before I got the rails I slept a little, then woke to find myself in a puddle about two inches deep."

Custer slogged on until the afternoon of March 31, when a courier appeared. A mixed enemy force led by Maj. Gen. George Pickett had attacked Sheridan at Dinwiddie, and Sheridan needed Custer's division at the front. Leaving Wells behind to accompany the wagons, Custer galloped ahead, Pennington's and Capehart's brigades with him in the muck and mire. Reaching the Union position, he ordered the brigades to dismount and fall in with the Reserve Brigade and the 2nd Cavalry Division, under Maj. Gen. George Crook.

As Custer's men prepared to meet the enemy behind hastily constructed barricades, many of the blue troopers sported red silk cravats around their collars in admiration of their commander. Custer himself carried a new guidon, hand sewn by Libbie. It was a red and blue swallow tail with large crossed sabers—the insignia of the cavalry— on both sides. "Several vigorous efforts were made to displace us from our position," Custer wrote of the Confederate onslaught. Eventually sensing an opportunity, Custer launched a counterattack.

The 3rd Cavalry Division broke through the Confederate position in this area at Sailor's Creek. (dd)

Pennington and Capehart drove Pickett back "handsomely until their supports were reached and they were enabled to make a stand." His men exhausted, Custer ordered them back to the safety of the Federal position.

On April Fool's Day, Sheridan, in coordination with Maj. Gen. Governeur Warren's V Corps, determined to finish off Pickett. After the fight at Dinwiddie Court House, Pickett had withdrawn to a crossroads known as Five Forks. With orders to form on Sheridan's left, Custer moved his men across country, marching parallel to White Oak Creek. Reaching his assigned position, Custer formed a juncture with Devin on his right. "Heavy lines of earth-works were discovered, extending for miles in either direction along our front. . . . [E]very point seemed to be strongly manned," he remembered. Once again, the division dismounted to probe Pickett's position, and the blue troopers maintained a desultory fire throughout the day.

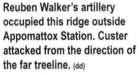

Reuben Walker's artillery occupied this ridge outside Appomattox Station. Custer attacked from the direction of the far treeline. (dd)

As darkness approached, Custer received word that Sheridan was ready to attack. Following a brief survey of the Confederate position, Custer decided to send Pennington forward on foot while

The Confederate wagon train stretched along the Richmond-Lynchburg Stage Road around Appomattox Court House. Elements from the 15th New York Cavalry reached the court house late in the fighting. During a brief skirmish in the darkness, the Empire Staters lost their colonel, Augustus Root. (kb-d)

Wells and Capehart launched a mounted attack into the Confederate flank. Bugles sounded up and down the line as Custer gave the order to advance. "Before the enemy could shift . . . my columns had pushed past the extreme right of his line and were moving rapidly to place themselves directly in rear of his position," Custer remembered. Sheridan's concentrated assault overwhelmed Pickett, and the Confederates collapsed under the weight. "The pursuit was maintained over a distance of six miles and only ended on account of darkness," he wrote.

Sheridan's capture of Five Forks put the Southside Railroad squarely in Union hands. Inspired by the success, Grant launched an army-wide assault early the next morning. Below Petersburg, elements of the VI Corps broke through the Confederate line and forced General Lee to abandon Petersburg and Richmond and head west. It was not long before the Union armies shook out in pursuit.

On April 3, Custer encountered enemy cavalry at Namozine Church. Holding the Confederates in front, he launched a flank assault that forced them to retreat. Colonel Wells, with elements of the 8th New York, ably turned back a counterattack. Custer then divided his division, sending the brigades to follow the retreating cavalry. This running fight lasted several hours before Custer called off the pursuit after encountering a strong infantry line.

After their engagement, the 3rd Cavalry Division marched on, reaching Jetersville on April

5. Next morning it headed west and encountered Confederate infantry led by Lt. Gen. Richard S. Ewell. This chance meeting, east of Farmville along Sailor's Creek, prompted an immediate attack by the Federals. In cooperation with Crook's division, Custer launched several unsuccessful assaults against Ewell's right flank. Obstinate, Custer's cavalry went forward again, and combined with blows from the VI Corps on his left, finally broke Ewell's line. Ewell himself surrendered as the Confederates retreated from the field. Custer rode on the next day and encamped at Prince Edward Court House.

Saddling up again on the morning of April 8, Custer and his division resumed their march. Their pace continued without incident until the middle of the afternoon when Confederate stragglers began to appear. One in particular revealed incredibly interesting news. Taken before Custer, the Confederate soldier told him that supply trains waited for the Army of Northern Virginia ahead at Appomattox Station. Sheridan's scouts, operating out in front of the cavalry, had also reported similar information. Besides this tantalizing supply prize, Custer also realized that if he reached the depot ahead of the Confederates, he stood a good chance of blocking Lee's path to

The reconstructed courthouse at Appomattox now serves as the Visitor Center for the Appomattox Court House National Historic Site. The museum display inside includes a piece of the towel used as a white flag delivered to Custer on the morning of April 9, 1865. It also includes a 3rd Cavalry Division guidon. (dd)

the west—Custer determined to push his men forward. He immediately dispatched a staff officer to Merritt to inform him of his intentions and spurred away.

Upon his approach to Appomattox, Custer confirmed the intelligence to be correct. Three locomotives, along with a contingent of engineers under Col. Thomas M. R. Talcott, waited at the station. Talcott's men quickly fled, leaving the trains in the hands of the cavalry. Custer immediately sent the engines steaming back to Farmville.

He also found that Talcott was not the only Confederate force in the area. About a mile west of the station was an artillery battalion under Maj. Gen. Reuben Walker, supported by a cavalry brigade under Brig. Gen. Martin Gary. As shells began falling amidst the blue horsemen, Custer dismounted his brigades and sent his troopers forward. "We advanced up to the enemy's guns, they replying mostly with canister while we used pistols and carbines," wrote a Vermont cavalryman from Wells's brigade. A member of Capehart's brigade who had just arrived on the scene remembered the muzzle flashes "as reflected against the sky, resembled a furious storm of lighting."

"Custer maintained the fight by repeated charges, now on the right, now on the left, now in the center," observed a Union staff officer. Walker held on against repeated attacks; even darkness did not bring an end to the fighting.

Sometime after 9 p.m., Custer, ever aggressive, turned to one of his aides and yelled, "Those guns must be taken in five minutes." Word quickly spread among the ranks and a hearty cheer went up from the 3rd Division. Riding out in front of his line, Custer drew his saber and led his men forward. His men "advanced and swept everything" before them. "The enemy's position was abandoned and an indiscriminate mass of guns, caissons and baggage-trains captured," remembered a Union officer.

Custer's troopers streamed east in the direction of Appomattox Court House after the Confederates. Reaching the village, Custer called off his men and returned to the vicinity of the station, where Devin's and Crook's divisions had arrived to relieve Custer. Although it was after midnight, Custer visited the wounded in a makeshift hospital and then departed for a few hours' sleep. As he bedded down, Custer rested easy knowing that his men had performed their duty. The door west had been slammed shut, and Lee was in a trap. To Lee's front was Sheridan's cavalry and behind him lay the Army of the Potomac. The Appomattox River flowed to the north while blue infantry was closing in from the south.

Early on the morning of April 9, in an attempt to break out, Lee sent his men forward through Appomattox Court House in the direction of the station. His determined Confederate infantry pushed back Crook's horsemen and threatened to open a hole in the Union line. Hard pressed, Merritt ordered Custer to join in the engagement. Custer led his division around to the right while elements of the V and XXIV Corps arrived to relieve the cavalry. "The rebel army was at our mercy," Merritt recalled as the men in gray and butternut broke off the fight and withdrew. Steadily, gunfire began to subside, and a Confederate staff officer soon appeared on Custer's front bearing a white flag. Custer immediately dispatched a courier to inform Sheridan of the proposed truce.

A meeting was soon arranged between Robert E. Lee and Ulysses S. Grant. They met at the home of Wilmer McLean in the village, their armies staring at each other and awaiting its outcome. Custer dismounted. Reaching for his canteen, he pulled the stopper and took a long drink. As he did, a sudden feeling came over him, one he had not felt in years, not since he was at West Point. Thoughts of war seemed all at once, far, far away. Mounting again, he set out to find Alexander Pennington.

Together they rode over to the Confederate lines in search of an old academy classmate, Robert Cowan. When he appeared, Custer hollered out, "Hello, you damned red-headed rebel." The small party had barely begun their conversation when they received word to break up while Lee and Grant conferenced. Not giving the warning much heed, the group resumed their reminiscences about the old days. Soon, word spread through the ranks that Lee had surrendered at Wilmer McLean's house inside the village.

Souvenir hunters raided the home. Phil Sheridan was among them, and he managed to commandeer a piece of furniture from the parlor. He promptly sent it to Libbie; with it she received Sheridan's note saying, "My dear Madam—I respectfully present to you the small writing table on which the conditions for the surrender . . . were written." Sheridan continued, "Permit me to say there is scarcely an individual in our service who has contributed more to bring this about than your very gallant husband."

Alfred Waud sketched Custer receiving the flag of truce. (loc)

After the War

CHAPTER ELEVEN

George Armstrong Custer emerged from the Civil War as one of the most famous men in North America. Motivated by his own lackluster performance at West Point, through sheer hard work, Custer had pulled himself up by his bootstraps from second lieutenant to brevet major general. His actions at New Bridge impressed George McClellan. Brandy Station and Aldie later convinced Alfred Pleasonton that Custer was ready for additional responsibilities. When the opportunity for command came, Custer took advantage of it and performed exceptionally well.

What makes his rise even more remarkable is that prior to the Gettysburg campaign, Custer did not have any command experience. His service until that time was at the staff level. Furthermore, he was not able to benefit from the tutelage and mentorship of a superior officer from the mounted arm. He learned through basic experience and observation of others. Custer was judicious in his actions at Gettysburg, Buckland Mills, Tom's Brook and Waynesboro. He also understood the value of the traditional cavalry charge, which he successfully executed at Yellow Tavern.

The shock produced by this tactic also led to one of Custer's only blemishes during the war. At Trevilian Station, he failed to secure his flank and rear during his effort to capture Wade Hampton's wagon train. It nearly resulted in the annihilation

For George Custer, the Civil War ultimately ended at the Wilmer McClean House in Appomattox Court House. (dd)

Custer, in his famous uniform, photographed in May 1865. As the decade continued, Custer grew increasingly leery of military life and, by decade's end, began searching for a way out of the army. (loc)

or capture of his entire command. Custer, however, was ordered by Sheridan to move on the station that morning. He was likely aware of the cavalry chief's clash with Meade. If Sheridan did not have any qualms about questioning the leadership of the army commander, he certainly would not go easy on a subordinate who disobeyed a directive. Custer's conduct may have come from a healthy fear of Sheridan rather than recklessness.

This battle also bore out Custer's finest asset as an officer. Through his experiences in the early part of the war, he came to appreciate that adverse circumstances, such as combat, help motivate man's natural anxiety over death. He understood that leadership could serve as a counterbalance to these feelings. Custer recognized that if an officer distinguished himself to those he led, terror quite often turned into inspiration, a key element to success or survival on the battlefield. During this battle, Custer rescued a wounded trooper and recaptured a gun from Pennington's battery all under the eyes of his Wolverines. His actions helped them to hold their position until relief arrived.

The recognition of this basic truth motivated Custer to personally lead in battle, a duty not required by a brigade or division commander. Time and again, at Hunterstown, Gettysburg, Yellow Tavern, in the autumn of 1863 at Brandy Station and Tom's Brook, he led assaults. He knew his place and felt that his men must always see him. He came to embody the spirit of the cavaliers of old with his unique uniform, personal guidon and a band to play patriotic airs in battle. He exuded self-confidence, a character trait often confused with vanity and arrogance. Custer believed in himself, in his abilities and that he could achieve victory under any circumstance. To believe otherwise could ultimately lead to failure.

Peace did not last long for Custer. After service in Texas, he received a commission in the newly reorganized army as a lieutenant colonel in the newly created 7th U.S. Cavalry. His introduction to Indian warfare in Kansas, Nebraska and Colorado in the spring and summer of 1867 resulted in a court martial. Custer was charged with being absent without leave, using government wagons for private business and conduct prejudicial to good

A page of *Harper's Weekly* depicts three sketches related to the battle of the Washita. At top is the approach of the 7th Cavalry. In the center is Captain Louis Hamilton, grandson of Alexander Hamilton, who was killed in the battle. At the bottom is the regiment's charge into the village. (loc)

order and military discipline. Custer was found guilty and suspended from rank for one year with no pay.

The army's inability to suppress the tribes of the Southern Plains forced Sheridan, now in command of the Department of the Missouri, to commute Custer's sentence in September 1868. Back with his regiment, Custer prepared for a winter campaign. On November 27, Lieutenant Colonel Custer led his regiment in an attack on Black Kettle's Southern Cheyenne camp along the banks of the Washita River in present day Oklahoma. Custer captured the village, a large pony herd and a number of women and children. When other Cheyenne, Kiowa and Arapahos appeared from nearby villages and threatened to surround the regiment, he skillfully maneuvered his command out of danger and returned to his base camp.

In the spring of 1874, Custer and the 7th U.S. Cavalry were dispatched on an expedition into the Black Hills, a region considered sacred by the Sioux. The march confirmed the presence of gold in the region and led to the Great Sioux War of 1876. (nps, lbhbnm)

Custer's victory and opportunity for redemption was soon tainted by an accusation from Capt. Frederick Benteen that he had abandoned Maj. Joel Elliott at the Washita. During the attack, Elliott set off with several troopers in pursuit of fleeing Cheyenne. Elliott and his men were eventually wiped out by the Indians coming to Black Kettle's aid, their bodies mutilated. When Custer learned of Elliott's absence, he had dispatched Capt. Edward Myers in an attempt to locate the missing troopers, but by that time, Elliott and his men had been wiped out. Unwilling to sacrifice his regiment should he remain and continue the search, Custer withdrew.

The following spring, augmented by the 19th Kansas Volunteer Cavalry, Custer set out again, leading his men into the Texas Panhandle. Using diplomacy rather than force this time, the lieutenant colonel managed to secure the release of several white captives from the Cheyenne and induce the Cheyenne to return to their reservation.

In spite of this recent success, Custer was unhappy. Bitterness over his court martial lingered, and Benteen's criticism further exacerbated feelings he had struggled with since the days following Trevilian Station. The recent campaigns had convinced the veteran officer to seek a new assignment. When an application for Commandant of Cadets at West Point was turned down, Custer turned to several business ventures. Over the course of the next several years, he failed to establish enough capital to allow him to resign his commission. Despite these civilian explorations, military matters continued to draw Custer back into the field.

In the summer of 1873, Custer and his regiment accompanied surveyors from the Northern Pacific Railroad into Montana Territory. The following year, he marched into the Black Hills, part of the Great Sioux Reservation. His assignment was to locate a suitable location for an army post, but instead the expedition discovered gold. These new deposits promised to help an economy still struggling to recover from a recent financial panic. When the U.S. government offered to purchase the region, the Sioux refused. Frustrated, President Ulysses S. Grant's administration tried a different approach. A declaration was issued stating that all Sioux who

Custer, at center, in the Black Hills after a grizzly bear hunt. At left is his scout, Bloody Knife, who would be killed at the Little Bighorn. (loc)

did not come in to live on their reservations by January 31, 1876, would be considered hostile and dealt with accordingly by the War Department. Thousands of Lakota and Oglalla, under Sitting Bull and Crazy Horse, never reported.

Custer's expedition against the hostiles would be delayed. In March, he was summoned before a House Committee to testify on the actions of former Secretary of War William Belknap, who was being investigated for fraud. Custer's testimony, while hearsay, angered the administration. Infuriated by his actions, Grant ordered that Custer not accompany his regiment in the field. Only after the intercession of Philip Sheridan and the commander of the U.S. Army, William T. Sherman, did the President relent. Custer could go but under the direction of the commander of the Department of Dakota, Brig. Gen. Alfred Terry.

On May 17, 1876, Custer and the 7th U.S. Cavalry departed Fort Abraham Lincoln. Accompanied by Brigadier General Terry, the column headed west to find the hostiles and force them back. Several weeks after setting out, they discovered a trail that finally put them on to the Sioux. Terry formulated a plan to capture them and dispatched Custer up Rosebud Creek.

At his encampment on the first night of the march, Custer's attitude deeply disturbed a number of his officers. His recent involvement in the Belknap

Named after Capt. Thomas Weir—commander of Company D, 7th U.S. Cavalry, who led the attempt to locate Custer's battalion—the high hill in the center of the photograph is the farthest Reno's and Benteen's men advanced along the bluffs before warriors drove them back. (dd)

Known as Water Carrier's Ravine, troopers used this avenue of approach to the Little Bighorn River to retrieve water for their comrades and horses during the hilltop fight. (dd)

affair had only added to his ongoing frustration with army life, frustration compounded by his failure to find another vocation to support himself and Libbie. This burden had put a massive strain on him. His determination and self-assurance had left him. Custer's greatest strength as a commander was gone.

*   *   *

As Custer led his battalion forward, Major Reno continued to engage warriors coming out of the village. When pressure began to mount on his front, Reno pulled back to a strip of timber. With Sioux and Cheyenne closing in, he ordered a withdrawal. "The order was given . . . and away we went," remembered 1st Sgt. John Ryan. "As we cut through them, the fighting was hand to hand and it was death to anyone who fell from his horse or was wounded and not able to keep up with the command." The troopers managed to cross the river and reach the bluffs on the opposite side. There, they met Captain Benteen and his battalion, followed by the pack train.

Gunfire downstream soon drew Reno's and Benteen's attention. They moved north in an attempt to unite with Custer, only to be turned back by swarms of Sioux and Cheyenne. Forced to defend itself again, the battalion assumed a position on the bluffs. "I dismounted the men and had the horses and mules of the pack-train driven together in a depression, put the men on the crests of the hills making the depression, and had hardly done so when I was furiously attacked," Reno wrote. The engagement continued until well after dark. Once the firing subsided, the men "went to work with what tools we had . . . and commenced throwing up breastworks," Ryan wrote.

Around 2:30 a.m. on June 26, the battle resumed. The fire from the warriors was "murderous," Pvt. Thomas Coleman wrote. Throughout the course of the day, both Reno and Benteen led charges to push back the warriors. Surprisingly, the fighting slackened as the day wore on. Early in the afternoon, the warriors set fire to the grass in the valley below. Several hours later, the cavalrymen caught site of the entire village abandoning its camp. "It was like some Biblical exodus," Pvt. Charles Windolph remembered.

Still without any contact with Custer, the men settled in for an uneasy sleep. The next morning, they could see a dust cloud, and about 10 a.m., Brig. Gen. Alfred Terry arrived on the bluff. He carried with him grim news. Marching along the Yellowstone and to the Bighorn River, Terry and Col. John Gibbon had marched down the Little Bighorn only to discover a grisly sight. About five miles away, "heaped in ravines and upon knolls," lay Custer and his entire battalion—more than 200 men. "Of the movements of General Custer and the five companies under his immediate command scarcely anything is known," Terry wrote.

Time has further obscured Custer's exact actions, although one thing is certain. Unlike Amissville, Kearneysville, and even the Washita, this time, he was unable to get out of trouble.

Dedicated on August 14, 1929, the Reno-Benteen Memorial stands at the Hilltop Defense site where seven companies of the regiment held out until they were relieved by Alfred Terry and John Gibbon on June 27. (dd)

Epilogue

Everything is still now, and relatively quiet. A pleasant breeze rustles through the grass along the bluff, the rustle mingling with the chirps of birds and crickets. Occasionally, I can make out the current in the river below. Although alone, I am surrounded by questions that resonate through time and swirl around Custer's final actions.

Atop Sharpshooter Ridge, I take in the same view as Custer when he saw the village on the banks of the Little Bighorn. Behind me is Cedar Coulee, used by Custer to maneuver northward. I head out along the bluffs, pass over Weir Peaks, and steadily ascend into Medicine Tail Coulee. This massive ravine offered Custer a potential approach to the river. Shortly after trumpeter Martin departed, Custer divided his battalion. His old friend, Capt. George Yates, received Company E, the "Gray Horse Troop," and Yates's own Company F. Along with Company I, Capt. Myles Keogh was assigned Companies C and L.

Custer sent Yates to reconnoiter while he moved with Keogh above the coulee to Luce Ridge. There he could provide cover to Yates and have a clear line of sight on his back trail. I proceed on to the head of the coulee. Its expansive size overwhelms the view. Although the river

The Little Bighorn River provided a vital water source for Sitting Bull's village in the summer of 1876. (ldd)

ABOVE: Custer viewed the Sioux village, then located at the upper left of the photograph, from Sharpshooter Ridge along the bluffs above the Little Bighorn River. Warriors later used the ridge to engage Benteen's and Reno's battalions. (dd)

RIGHT: Custer led his battalion down Cedar Coulee, which feeds into Medicine Tail Coulee. (dd)

is ahead of me, I cannot see it. It is hidden by the banks and sagebrush. On the other side of Medicine Tail Ford stood the Cheyenne circle. Warriors on the opposite bank opened fire as Yates approached. The engagement was brief. Convinced the ford was guarded, Yates turned about and withdrew.

The two battalions reunited on Nye-Cartwright Ridge but a band of Cheyenne led by Wolf Tooth and Big Foot struck the battalions. Substantial volleys from Yates and Keogh eventually pressed them back. With the route below him blocked, Custer determined to move north.

Making my way out of Medicine Tail Coulee, I pass through Deep Coulee and over Greasy Grass Ridge until I reach Finley-Finckle Ridge. Up the ridge and to the east is another hill. Prominent and pronounced, it commands the surrounding terrain. When Custer reached that point above me, he detached Keogh to cover Benteen's approach. Keogh placed Company L there, commanded by Custer's brother-in-law, 1st Lt. James Calhoun. Elements of Company C deployed to the ridge I stand on. It bears the name of two company sergeants whose bodies were found here: Jeremiah Finley and August Finkle.

Second Lieutenant Henry Harrington may have also died somewhere nearby. He was one of three officers from Custer's battalion, along with 1st Lt. James Porter and 2nd Lt. James

Capt. George Yates's battalion advanced from the high ground in the distance down Medicine Tail Coulee toward the Little Bighorn River. (dd)

ABOVE: Nye-Cartwright Ridge: named for Col. Elwood Nye and R. G. Cartwright. Artifacts found here provide clues to Custer's movements in the latter stages of his engagement. This photo of the ridge was taken from the position of Company L. (dd)

LEFT: Following the repulse of Yates, warriors advanced up Deep Coulee to engage Custer's battalion. (dd)

Likely under Custer's direction, elements from Company C deployed on Finley-Finkle Ridge to protect Company L's flank. (dd)

Sturgis, whose remains were never identified. That morning, Capt. Tom Custer assumed the duties of aide-de-camp to his brother and passed company command to Harrington. Covering Company L's right flank, Harrington's men engaged warriors on Greasy Grass Ridge. Those warriors steadily pushed up the ridge and overwhelmed the troopers.

In the midst of Company C's position, marble headstones stare back at me in every direction. Placed across the landscape, they mark the spots where soldiers fell.

In May 1890, Capt. Owen Sweet and a contingent from the 25th U.S. Infantry erected headstones to mark the locations where troopers fell. These headstones are for Company C troopers on Finley-Finkle Ridge. They remain the most haunting sight on the battlefield. (dd)

Continuing beyond, I reach Calhoun Hill. Walking back from the crest, I find Calhoun's headstone. Behind it is one for 2nd Lt. John Crittenden, Calhoun's second in command. An officer in the 20th U.S. Infantry, Crittenden came to the regiment shortly before the expedition left Fort Abraham Lincoln. At the request of his family, Crittenden remained buried on the field. His remains were eventually reinterred in the national cemetery, less than a mile away.

Calhoun's right flank disintegrated when the troopers' line at Finley-Finkle Ridge collapsed. Slowly, the warriors began to close in. To their front, Calhoun and Crittenden had to contend with a force led by the Hunkpapa Sioux, Gall. Behind them, White Bull, a Miniconjou, and Crazy Horse, commanding Oglala, launched a charge that split Company L's contact with Company I and elements of Company C. They were soon swept away.

I enter a swale, and then to my right, the view opens up. Headstones are scattered about

Warriors used Greasy Grass Ridge as a firing platform to engage and eventually overrun troopers on Finley-Finkle Ridge. (dd)

Custer chose Calhoun Hill, here seen from Finley-Finkle Ridge, for his men because of its defensive advantage. (dd)

The headstones honor James Calhoun, foreground, and John Crittenden, background. Calhoun, the commander of Company L, married the Custer's sister, Margaret Custer, on March 7, 1872. After the battle, cartridge cases found underneath Calhoun's body, along with his watch, were returned to his widow. Crittenden, originally assigned to the 20th U.S. Infantry, was detached to Company L prior to the opening of the spring campaign. He was identified after the battle by his glass eye, the result of a hunting accident several years before the battle. Like Calhoun, his timepiece was also eventually recovered and returned to his family. He rests today in the National Cemetery at the Little Bighorn. (dd)

the landscape. Starting in a ravine, they stretch, singly, in threes and fours and larger groups, along the eastern face of what is known today as Battle Ridge. With the fall of Calhoun Hill, the remainder of Keogh's battalion was overrun and perished in the prairie before me. Some of those who survived stubbornly fought their way to Custer while others ran for their lives in panic-stricken horror.

When he left Keogh, Custer galloped along Battle Ridge. He still hoped to find another crossing and anticipated Benteen's arrival. Reaching a high knoll, he dispatched Yates with Company F farther north to locate a ford. Yates rode on for a short distance until he collided with large numbers of Sioux. Steadily, his troopers were pushed back to ground now occupied by the National Cemetery. As more warriors concentrated on Yates, Custer decided to send 1st Lt. Algernon Smith's Company E to his aid. Smith directed his men toward a basin below the ridge, Deep Ravine. There they collided with

Lame White Man and his Cheyenne. The assault crippled both companies, and the remnants pulled back to the knoll. Custer's desperation mounted as he watched Keogh get overrun. Hope slipped away and soldiers shot their horses for cover.

Company I and the remnants of Companies C and L were destroyed on the east face of Battle Ridge. (dd)

I rest my hands on wrought iron rail erected in the shadow of a monument to the 7th Cavalry. Just feet away, Custer's body was found on June 28 by members of his regiment detailed to bury the dead. Before me, enclosed by the fence, are headstones for those who died with him.

I wonder what it was like here in those final, desperate moments as the men shot their horses to use for cover. Custer had to have watched his defenses crumble below him on Finley-Finkle Ridge and Calhoun Hill, where his brother-in-law's command was swept away. Yet, even with that defensive position gone, Custer was still surrounded by family. Tom was with him, as was his brother Boston and his nephew, Harry Reed.

Along with the soldiers' headstones, red granite markers scattered throughout the battlefield show where Sioux and Cheyenne warriors fell. Lame White Man marker is on the right. A Northern Cheyenne, Lame White Man led an assault that was critical in the collapse and destruction of Custer's battalion. (dd)

Did words pass between them as they chambered another round? Or did they just exchange glances before the swift and brutal end? Did they get even that last opportunity to say goodbye?

This place draws me in, and time nearly comes to a halt. The place is haunting and enshrouded in the unknown. I seem to have answered many questions about what happened, what Custer planned and the decisions he made—yet, some answers elude me. The mystery surrounding what happened to him and his battalion will remain, as James H. Kidd wrote, "until the dead are called upon to give up their secrets."

Years of being in the field made Custer look older than thirty six when he died at the Little Bighorn. (loc)

Thirty-two soldiers were found around Last Stand Hill. The headstones inside the enclosed fence below the 7th Cavalry Monument mark the places where the men fell and were interred after the battle. Custer's headstone bears the black shield in the center and marks the spot where he was buried. Along with the other officers, his remains were disinterred, in July 1877, for reburial elsewhere. He rests next to Libbie in the cemetery at West Point. Deep Ravine can be seen at the upper center of the picture. To the upper right is a section of the National Cemetery. (dd)

Tom Custer

APPENDIX A
BY DANIEL T. DAVIS

The third child of Emmanuel and Maria Custer to survive childhood, Thomas Ward compiled a military record that rivaled that of his older brother. At the outbreak of the Civil War, Tom enlisted on September 2, 1861 in the 21st Ohio Infantry and fought at the Battle of Stones River. Beginning in April 1863, Tom was detached from the regiment and served on escort duty for Brig. Gens. James Negley, John Palmer and Maj. Gen. Ulysses S. Grant.

Through Autie's efforts, Tom was discharged in the fall of 1864 and received an officer's commission in the 6th Michigan Cavalry. He arrived at the Army of the Shenandoah shortly after the Battle of Cedar Creek and was reassigned to serve as an aide-de-camp on Autie's staff. Tom was present at the battles of Waynesboro, Dinwiddie Court House and Five Forks. On April 3, 1865, he finally had an opportunity to display his mettle.

During the engagement at Namozine Church, Tom captured the flag of the 2nd North Carolina Cavalry. Three days later at Sailor's Creek, he participated in the 3rd Cavalry Division's assault on the Confederate position. Once again, he personally captured an enemy battle flag but was shot in the face. He survived the wound and for his gallantry received a Medal of Honor for each act.

In September 1866, Tom received a commission as first lieutenant in Autie's regiment, the 7th U.S. Cavalry. He fought at the Washita and served on the Yellowstone and Black Hills expeditions. In December 1875, he was promoted to captain in time for the upcoming summer expedition against the Sioux. Tom's body was found close to Autie's on Last Stand

Built fourteen years before the beginning of the Civil War, Namozine Church survived the brief engagement between Union and Confederate cavalry on April 3, 1865. In the open fields nearby, Tom Custer earned the first of his two Medals of Honor. (dd)

Hill. Troopers of the 7th Cavalry interred them next to each other on the crest below the knoll. His remains were exhumed in July 1877 and re-interred in the Fort Leavenworth National Cemetery.

A photograph of Thomas Custer taken in 1872 wearing his Medals of Honor. (nps, lbhbnm)

MEDAL OF HONOR CITATIONS
Thomas W. Custer

Rank and Organization:
Second Lieutenant, Company B, 6th Michigan Cavalry

First Award
Place and Date: Namozine Church, Va.,
April 3, 1865
Citation: *Capture of a flag*

Second Award
Place and Date: Sailor Creek, Va., April 1865
Citation: *2nd Lt. Custer leaped his horse over the enemy's works and captured 2 stands of colors, having his horse shot from under him and receiving a severe wound*

Tom Custer's body was found some twenty feet from his older brother's after the battle of the Little Bighorn. The two were buried next to each other in the same grave below the crest of Last Stand Hill. Tom was disinterred in July 1877 and rests today in the Fort Leavenworth National Cemetery. (dd)

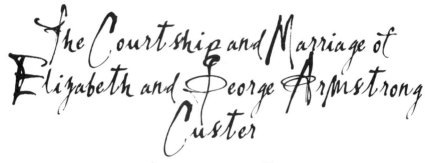

The Courtship and Marriage of Elizabeth and George Armstrong Custer

APPENDIX B
BY ASHLEY WEBB

The romance and devotion detailed throughout the twelve-year marriage of Elizabeth and George Armstrong Custer continues to intrigue historians, especially as Elizabeth idealized their flawed but loving partnership after Custer's fateful death. Of their marriage, Elizabeth wrote, "I lived through a blaze of sunshine for twelve years," and when Captain William McCaskey relayed the news concerning Custer's death, Elizabeth declared that "the windows of life that let in the sunshine" closed forever. Custer's tragic end at the battle of Little Bighorn fueled his wife's dedication to his memory, building a faultless hero that she aimed would outlive his critics and enemies. Although Elizabeth's portrayal of Custer and their marriage in her three memoirs *Boots and Saddles, Following the Guidon*, and *Tenting the Plains* glorify their adventurous life together throughout the American West, their courtship and marriage were full of separation, rumor, and transparent confessions of conscience.

Elizabeth Clift Bacon (Libbie), the only surviving child of Judge Daniel S. Bacon and Eleanor Sophia Page, was born on April 8, 1842, in Monroe, Michigan. When Libbie's mother died of dysentery in 1854, Libbie's bereft and grieving father sent his daughter to live with her aunt while he mourned alone. Eventually, Judge Bacon remarried and enrolled Libbie in the Young Ladies Seminary and Collegiate Institute, also known as Boyd's Seminary, where she learned the art of Victorian conversation and flirtation. She graduated as valedictorian in the spring of 1862.

Libbie's chestnut-colored hair, petite stature, and gray-blue eyes drew many suitors, making her a local belle among Union soldiers, Monroe visitors, and eligible townsmen. In that summer after graduation, Libbie courted at least five men; each man won her father's favor but not Libbie's heart. Although the Civil

Autie and Libbie were married at the First Presbyterian Church of Monroe, Michigan. (fa)

At times tumultuous, the twelve year marriage of Autie and Libbie Custer has also become a subject of romantic myth. (loc)

War didn't make a big impact on her life, the constant entertaining of Union soldiers romanticized the idea of marrying a "gilt-striped and Button kind." Judge Bacon disapproved of soldiers, writing that military men "were charming as admirers, but not to be taken seriously."

In the fall of 1862, 20-year-old Libbie attended a Thanksgiving party at Boyd's Seminary, and was introduced to Capt. George Armstrong Custer, "Autie" as he was known to friends and family. The two had grown up down the street from each other, yet because of their social and religious circles were never acquaintances. Their meeting was brief but certainly made lasting impressions on each. Libbie later wrote, "With the critical and exacting eye of a girl I decided I would never like him no matter how attentive he was." Autie, however, became smitten with Libbie immediately, learning her daily schedule in order to accompany her on errands. After Christmas, his walks past her house seemed upward of "forty times a day," and whenever she put her "nose out of doors," Custer was there to meet her.

Around New Year's Day of 1863, Autie discussed marriage with Libbie, an event which she refused. Judge Bacon, belatedly learning of Libbie's infatuation with the young captain, forbade her to see him. Her father's approval mattered more to Libbie, and she seemed to take his adamant opposition of Custer to heart. While Libbie visited friends in Ohio, her father wrote to her of his disapproval. She retorted that "I did it all for you. . . . . You will never see me in the street with him again. . . . I told him never to meet me, and he has the sense to understand. But I did not promise to never see him again. But I will not cause you any more trouble, be sure." Despite her father's dismissal of Custer, Libbie and Autie continued a quiet courtship, even as Autie flaunted a public relationship with Libbie's seminary rival Fanny Fifield.

Later in life, Libbie declared that Autie's courtship with Fanny was intended to create gossip and to dispel rumors concerning herself and Custer since her father had forbidden them to see each other. Libbie, nonetheless, often voiced her feelings about Autie's attraction to Fanny in her personal journal. She wrote, "C—knowing the low-minded girl as he does, should wish to marry her." She continued at a later date that Autie "had no business to write the passionate messages he has about me & to me when he has been writing so constantly & lovelike to Fan. He is nothing to me. He never will be." When Custer left

Monroe in April of 1863, his and Libbie's relationship was at a standstill.

Despite Libbie's frustrations concerning her relationship with Custer, she and Autie continued some semblance of a courtship throughout the rest of 1863, writing letters through a mutual friend in Monroe. Libbie needed to keep her pledge to her father, but her affection for Custer grew. She wrote in her journal, "I was not in love—yes I was, perhaps . . . but I feel that it is proof that I do not really love for how could I silence so soon feelings that are always so deep?" In addition to his letters through their go-between, Custer continued corresponding with Fanny, much to Libbie's disappointment. Even this early in their relationship, Libbie remained frank with Custer concerning the trail of women that he left in his wake. At one point, when Autie attempted to embrace Libbie, she declared that "she was no Fanny Fifield or Helen W. either, another young woman of questionable virtue with whom his name was linked." The letters relayed through their friend reveal Libbie's jealousy and the constant reassurance that Custer offered to convince Libbie of his love for her.

Soon after the young captain was promoted to brigadier general, a leg wound in a second battle at Brandy Station earned Custer a fifteen-day leave in Monroe. During this short period, Libbie and Autie met frequently, and she decided once and for all that "every other man seems so ordinary beside my own bright particular star." Her previous misgivings about their relationship were quieted, and upon acceptance from her father, their engagement was announced. Custer pushed for a winter 1864 wedding, knowing he'd have some kind of furlough then, but Libbie pleaded for a longer engagement. She wasn't ready to trade her youthful freedom "for the myriad and confining duties of running a household." Autie begged her family and friends to persuade Libbie to consent: "Cannot you threaten her, or use your influence to induce her to do as she ought?" After a month of imploring, Libbie gave in, settling on an ostentatious evening wedding to take place on February 9, 1864.

Immediately after the wedding, the happy couple traveled through Ohio and New York, with a special

Libbie Custer unveiled the equestrian statue of her husband, *Sighting the Enemy*, in Monroe, Michigan. Standing next to her on the podium is President William Howard Taft. (nps, lbhbnm)

stopover at West Point. While there, Libbie endured the first of "many silent seasons," again making her question Autie and his love for her. While he reminisced and met with former instructors, cadets escorted Libbie down Lovers' Walk, where one professor happened to kiss Custer's bride. Upon learning this, Autie "turned into an incarnate thundercloud," refusing to listen to any of her explanations regarding the situation. At his withdrawal, Libbie, agitated at his silence, remarked, "Well, you left me with them, Autie!" Libbie and Autie made a pact to "'fess up' to anything that [their] consciences suggested that the other would not approve."

From New York, the newlyweds traveled to Washington. As soon as they had arrived, though, Libbie described that "telegrams came, following one another in quick succession, asking him to give up the rest of his leave of absence, and hasten without an hour's delay to the front. I begged so hard not to be left behind. . . . The result was that I found myself . . . in an isolated Virginia farmhouse, finishing my honeymoon alone." Throughout Custer's career, separation became a constant for Libbie, regardless of her attempts to remain with her husband. At one point, she remarked, "There were so often, in those days of oft-occurring separations, repeated honeymoons." During the first two years of the young couple's marriage, the Civil War caused many of these separations. While in Washington, Libbie worked methodically to help advance Autie's career—meeting with important dignitaries, generals, and even President Lincoln—to solidify her husband's reputation within the Union army. Her skilled socializing worked, but also created several enemies for both her and Autie in the process.

When the couple wasn't separated, Libbie focused on reforming many of Autie's flaws, including his gambling addiction and his lack of devotion to God. Autie's impetuous tendencies and get-rich-quick schemes often backfired, leaving Autie in difficult financial situations. Libbie learned to make her own clothes, copying the fashions of the day, while Custer chased the next game of faro, horse races, and even the next contract within the Army. It was the latter of the three that often separated Libbie and Autie. After the Civil War, Custer often traveled East in search of opportunities, eventually deciding that there was no better position than in the cavalry.

After the Civil War, Autie moved with Gen. Philip H. Sheridan from New Orleans out to Texas, but Custer's position was mustered out, causing the couple to move back to Monroe. Libbie stayed with her parents, while Autie traveled east to Washington and to New York City to garner prospects for work. While in New York City, though, Autie detailed in letters to his wife his numerous excursions and socializing with other women. Autie formed attachments with actress Maggie Mitchell, opera singer Clara Louise Kellogg, and frequently escorted two of Libbie's friends to masquerades. In one letter, he confessed that he and several West Point officers one night visited a number of "pretty-girl-waitress saloons," before wandering out to flirt with prostitutes—"'Nymphes du Pave' they are called. Sport alone was our object." During the same trip, Autie described a guest at a party that he attended: the baroness "wore a very handsome satin, and oh so low. I sat beside her on a sofa and 'I have not seen such sights since I was weaned.'" Three months later, Autie remained in New York City galivanting around the city, while Libbie took care of her ailing father. Judge Bacon passed away on May 18, 1866.

Libbie Custer, photographed shortly after the turn of the century, still wore mourning clothes. (nps, lbhbnm)

Libbie wrote off Custer's absence from the funeral as having "to be in New York for a few days."

While rumors about Autie's infidelity spread, Libbie refused to acknowledge the mixed messages within their marriage. In 1867, Autie confessed to Libbie, "You know I promised never to give you fresh cause for regret by attentions paid to other girls, so firmly has this become my creed and my resolve, thus my determination, carried forward by my love for you." At another point, he wrote, "All the women are but as mere toys compared to you." Regardless of his reassurances, the separations continued to happen, including another lengthy estrangement early in 1871. Custer again traveled East to New York, visiting with acquaintances, including rekindling the friendship he had with Clara Kellogg. In several letters to Libbie, he detailed how Clara had repeatedly asked him back to her dressing room after shows, to which he declined at first, but later confessed, "I could only open the door a few inches . . . as she was dishabille," but he did catch "occasional glimpses of a beautifully turned leg encased in purple tights." On the same trip, Autie proclaimed, "Darling Standby . . . The old Irish servant who takes care of my room looks at me with suspicion when I return, sometimes not till morning, the bed not having been touched," but he was quick to defend himself saying, "she believes I do not pass my nights in the most reputable manner. In fact, circumstances, as she sees them, are against me."

In spite of the cognizant confessions regarding Custer's infidelity during their separations, along with rumors concerning Autie's relationship with a Cheyenne woman named Monahsetah while on the Plains, Libbie and Autie seemed to have a happy relationship throughout their time in the Dakotas. Libbie followed Autie wherever she could, making a home for them out of the meager supplies and furnishings available to them. Throughout the 1870s, the Custers enjoyed inviting friends out West to stay with them and often concocted social affairs for individuals in the 7th Cavalry. Libbie encouraged Autie to write, and he published *My Life on the Plains* in early 1876, with hopes of signing contracts to speak in a lecture circuit across the East Coast. This hope was cut short, though, as Custer's luck had run out: Autie did not return from his last campaign against the Sioux and Cheyenne Indians in June of that year.

At her husband's death, Libbie felt as if her entire world had ended. Rumors of Custer's insubordination, rashness, and selfishness besieged the newspapers after Little Bighorn, and the glory she felt he deserved was on the verge of collapse. Additionally, Libbie was forced to realize the extent of her husband's debt. Autie had taken a number of unprofitable risks during the last few years of his life, and with his death, Libbie was burdened with over $13,000 in debt. This left a lot for the young widow to contemplate, including how she would be able to support herself from her husband's meager estate.

On her return to Monroe in the days after the fateful battle, Libbie decided that the rest of her life would be dedicated to restoring "the luster of her Autie's damaged reputation." Libbie became a constant defender of Custer's honor, hoping to outweigh the negativity and speculation from the slanderous newspapers, asserting that "Custer was not at fault for the disaster; therefore, someone else must be." After moving to New York City, Libbie took a part-time position as a secretary of a women's organization in order to make some kind of life of her own—she eventually retired in June of 1882 when Congress awarded her her husband's pension—but over time, increasingly, she chose to put her husband in the spotlight, writing three memoirs idealizing her relationship with her husband and romanticizing their life together. Her books were well received, and she became popular on the literary lecture circuit. She traveled the world giving lectures and talks, fighting to keep Custer's memory in the forefront as a hero. She never slowed in her memorials and tributes, and she hoped to see the day "when tradition and history will be so mingled that no one will be able to separate them." Elizabeth Bacon Custer passed away four days short of her 91st birthday on April 4, 1933.

Libbie and Autie's relationship, despite its problems, was one of love and devotion. It was flawed, often complicated, and not much like what Libbie portrayed in her memoirs. The true relationship between the couple, which is widely detailed in their letters to each other, is much more interesting than what Libbie portrayed. The rumors of infidelity and confessions of conscience caused rifts and constant separations throughout their twelve-year marriage, yet the partnership between the two remained strong, even after Autie's death.

Based in Roanoke, Virginia, Ashley Webb *works as a freelance museums registrar and collections specialist. She has her own blog, Blue Ridge Vintage, highlighting the history of everyday objects.*

Custer in Memory
APPENDIX C
BY PAUL ASHDOWN

In 1952, my parents enrolled me as a member of the Young Readers of America, a new subscription service sponsored by the Book of the Month Club. Each month, for a charge of $1.50 plus shipping costs, the club provided a selection from the Random House publishing company's Landmark Books, a series of historical volumes intended for readers between the ages of 9 and 15. Some 70,000 of us reportedly were reading Landmark Books by the end of the first year. Each book came with an attractively illustrated dust jacket, an explanatory pamphlet, and a personal letter from the author.

The first book in the series, *The Voyages of Christopher Columbus*, had been published in 1950, and other titles quickly followed. The first book I received, number 20 in the series and published in 1951, was *Custer's Last Stand*, written by the famous World War II correspondent Quentin Reynolds, and illustrated by Frederick T. Chapman. Some 180 titles eventually were published in the series. Just about all of them found their way into home and school libraries where they provided primary source material for an untold number of assigned book reports.

My copy of *Custer's Last Stand* long ago disappeared from my bookshelves, but I recently replaced it with another volume, a 13th printing, that I found in a used bookstore. As I again read the first chapter, titled "A Boy Has a Dream," I could only wonder what I had made of George Armstrong

This monument to Custer stands on the back streets of Hardin, Montana, several miles from his last battlefield. (dd)

Dedicated on the 145th anniversary of the battle, this monument to Custer and the trooper who saved him, Sgt. Norvill Churchill, stands behind the Union position at Hunterstown. (dd)

Custer's rush to glory while first reading of him during my youth in the midst of the Korean War and a presidential election campaign that would bring another famous general to the White House.

Evidently the same question troubled Tom Engelhardt, who, having completed a book that involved "a journey to a long ignored childhood land," felt moved "to find a used copy of Quentin Reynolds's children's book *Custer's Last Stand*, and to see, so many years later, the familiar illustration of the sole survivor of Custer's command, Myles Keogh's horse Comanche, proud head bowed, being led away by a soldier. In the flyleaf of my present copy," Engelhardt continued, "is the penciled comment, dated 1956-57 in a young hand, 'One of the deep moving books, I thoroughly enjoyed', and in another, even younger hand, simply 'I LOVE AUTIE' (Custer's nickname). My sentiments of the time exactly." I wondered if Engelhardt and I, both born in 1944, might have found each other's book, and whether it was my young hand that had written I LOVE AUTIE in 1952.

While working on my own book about Custer with my co-author Ed Caudill, I came across Daniel Dyer's review of another Custer book in the *Cleveland Plain Dealer*. Dyer, who must be a little younger, said he was about 10 when he read *Custer's Last Stand*, "a perfect book for an Oklahoma boy like me intoxicated by the surfeit of cowboy shows on 1950s TV. Reynolds ignited a George Armstrong Custer brushfire in my imagination." Possibly Dyer added the comments to Engelhardt's copy, or he has my book. How many others of us owe a debt to Reynolds, or one of the many authors who have been fanning that brushfire for the last 150 years?

A peculiar autobiographical imperative seems to be prevalent throughout the Custer literature, no more so than in the work of one of the leading Custer scholars, Robert M. Utley, former chief historian of the National Park Service. I had a pleasant conversation with Utley in Washington, D.C., in the mid-1990s, and have enjoyed many of his fine books. He spent so much time writing and talking about Custer during his career that when he published a memoir in 2004 he justifiably titled it *Custer and Me*.

In the preface to his book on the Last Stand, Nathaniel Philbrick says he first learned about Custer at the Battle of the Little Bighorn "not in school but at the movies." For Philbrick, born in 1956, Custer was "the deranged maniac of *Little Big Man*." For his parents' generation, Custer was "the noble hero played by Errol Flynn in *They Died with Their Boots On*. In both instances, Custer was more cultural lightning rod than historical figure, an icon instead of a man."

And so, we come to Custer already bewitched by the books and movies that shape us, and have to free ourselves from the mythologies that have been accruing since Libbie Custer took possession of her husband's memory, at that time ordered and shaped by Custer himself long before his death at the Little Bighorn. Libbie lived until 1933, celebrated until the end for her devotion to her husband's memory if not for her objectivity. With the publication of Frederic F. Van de Water's *Glory Hunter: A Life of General Custer* in 1934, the theretofore scattered attacks on Custer's legacy escalated into a literary and historical Little Bighorn. The battle has ebbed and flowed ever since, depending on what story the country wanted to hear about Custer and about Native Americans.

I grew up in Dade County, Florida, renamed Miami-Dade County in 1997. Not many people in Miami or anywhere else in Florida could have identified Major Francis Dade, for whom the county was later named, let alone discussed the Dade Massacre of 1835. Major Dade and 110 soldiers were ambushed by Seminoles in what precipitated the Second Seminole War. Only a couple of soldiers survived. It took months before more soldiers found what was left of the bodies on the battlefield north of the Withlacoochee River near what is now Bushnell, about 60 miles north of Tampa. The massacre was a national news story for a few months until it was pushed out of the news by the Battle of the Alamo, then forgotten.

Why do we know about Custer's Last Stand but not the Dade Massacre? What's the difference? We don't even know for sure if there was a "last stand" as visualized in the famous Anheuser Busch lithograph *Custer's Last Fight* that hung above the bar in some 150,000 American taverns. We do

A *Harper's Weekly* sketch captured the popular and public image of Custer at war. (loc)

know that Major Dade was shot dead off his horse in the first blast. Many historians think Custer also may have fallen long before the bloody conclusion of the battle that made him immortal, but that's not the way popular history wants to remember him.

One of many reasons Custer endures is that his death occurred in 1876, 41 years after the Dade Massacre and just as the nation was celebrating its centennial. Custer's defeat at the Little Bighorn went off the script, a counter-narrative to the triumphal conquest of the West. By that time a true national press was in the process of creation. Reporters were giving the masses a diet of Wild West stories facilitated by the telegraph and photography. Custer already had posed for 155 photographs, making him one of the most recognizable Americans of his time. Mark Kellogg, a reporter for the *Bismarck Tribune* in the Dakota Territory as well as a stringer for the *New York Herald* and the Associated Press died with Custer on the battlefield. Kellogg's dispatches during the campaign had created a sensation. Clement Lounsberry, publisher of the *Bismarck Tribune*, interviewed survivors of the campaign and telegraphed some 15,000 words to the New York press to break the news of the Little Bighorn disaster.

From that moment on Custer became a recognizable cultural symbol. The 89th Academy Awards ceremony, in 2017, collapsed into farce when the best picture award went to the wrong film. A newspaper columnist imagined comparable historical embarrassments, reserving the best for Custer, named the winner at the Little Bighorn because Buffalo Bill lost his reading glasses. That's no more absurd than recent cartoons showing Custer succumbing to technological distractions: sending his last tweets and taking a selfie at Little Bighorn as the "redskins" close in. *Los Angeles Times* cartoonist David Horsey imagined the yellow-haired dandy Donald Trump as Custer riding to Sioux territory to spur the Dakota Access Oil Pipeline project. You couldn't get away with any of these images unless a significant number of people could identify Custer as a symbol of vainglorious defeat.

What gets lost in all this is the Civil War Custer, the golden-boy general who fought it out from Bull Run to Appomattox, leading every charge "with a whoop and a shout," in the words of Abraham Lincoln. Always in the thick of the fight, he even stole the show at the Grand Review of the Army of the Potomac in Washington when his horse, Don Juan, bolted in front of the reviewing stand on Pennsylvania Avenue. Ever flamboyant, Custer, abruptly hatless and with yellow hair streaming, deftly restrained the mount, creating an irresistible tableau for journalists and biographers. The moment all but defined Custer's battles for generations fascinated by the Civil War but was lost to the wider public that judged Custer only for what happened on the last afternoon of his life. The burden of Custer's Little Bighorn defeat shrouded Custer's achievements at Gettysburg, Yellow Tavern, Williamsburg, Trevilian Station, Cedar Creek and Waynesboro.

GENERAL CUSTERS DEATH STRUGGLE.
The Battle of the Little Big Horn.

Not much of this even got into *Custer's Last Stand.* Reynolds covered the Civil War in just 12 pages. He seemed to lose interest in the war altogether after Autie became a general and got married. "It was a long war, and he saw plenty of action, but finally it was all over and he led his troops in the victory parade in Washington," was the way Reynolds summed it up. Then Custer went out West and the Civil War was forgotten. But not Custer.

Custer's last battle at the Little Bighorn was depicted in an 1878 lithograph by the Pacific Art Company. (loc)

PAUL ASHDOWN *is a professor emeritus of journalism at the University of Tennessee. He worked as a journalist after receiving bachelor's and master's degrees in journalism at the University of Florida. He studied broadcasting and popular culture at Bowling Green State University in his Ph.D. program. His interest in the Civil War probably began when he read MacKinlay Kantor's Gettysburg, Number 23 in the Landmark Book series, in 1952.*

Officer Remembered
APPENDIX D
BY DANIEL T. DAVIS

The passage of time tends to obscure our view of certain events or individuals. Like the Sioux and Cheyenne warriors who surrounded and vanquished his battalion, George Armstrong Custer continues to have myth swirl around his life. The "Boy General's" demise on that southeastern Montana knoll catapulted him to new heights in popular memory and has overshadowed his contemporaries.

For instance, the popular image of Custer today depicts him outnumbered and single-handedly fending off Jeb Stuart's Confederates on July 3, 1863, at Gettysburg. Although Custer played an important part in the engagement, Brig. Gen. David Gregg held tactical command on what became known as East Cavalry Field. Custer operated under Gregg's direction and in concert with one of Gregg's brigades under Col. John M. McIntosh.

Similarly, Custer was not the premier soldier in the post-bellum regular army. While he did enjoy some success on the Southern Plains, officers such as Ranald MacKenzie and Nelson Miles far surpassed any of Custer's accomplishments. If not for his death, Custer may have faded from public conscience.

That does not mean Custer was not a good officer, which is attested by his achievements in the Civil War. He built his success by adopting a particular tactic. During the height of the engagement at Gettysburg, Custer led the 1st Michigan Cavalry in an assault against Confederate brigades led by Brig. Gens. Wade Hampton and Fitzhugh Lee. As the momentum of the charge began to dissipate, elements from other Union regiments, the 1st New Jersey, 3rd Pennsylvania, and 5th Michigan struck at the gray flanks. This combined weight caused the Confederate formation to break apart.

The idea of striking an enemy's front while simultaneously attacking the flank made an impression on Custer. He utilized this concept twice more during the war. Both instances were as a division commander. At Tom's Brook, in October, 1864,

Custer's Knoll at Little Bighorn dd)

Custer sent elements from Cols. William Wells's and Alexander C. M. Pennington's brigades against Maj. Gen. Thomas Rosser's position on the Back Road. As the Union troopers moved forward, the 8th New York, 22nd New York, and 18th Pennsylvania turned the Confederate left. The result was arguably Custer's finest battlefield triumph.

A few months later, in March 1865, Custer employed the tactic against the remnants of Lt. Gen. Jubal Early's Army of the Valley in the battle of Waynesboro. Custer pushed Wells and Pennington, along with the brigade of Col. Henry Capehart, against Brig. Gen. Gabriel Wharton's division front to occupy Confederate attention. Meanwhile, the 1st Connecticut, 2nd Ohio, and 3rd New Jersey slipped around the left end of Wharton's position. "So sudden was our attack and so great was the enemy's surprise that but little time was offered for resistance," Custer wrote. Wharton's division collapsed and the Confederate retreat quickly escalated into a rout.

Perhaps these battles passed through Custer's mind on the morning of June 25, 1876. Although it will never be certain, his plan at the Little Bighorn closely mirrored his previous battles. Major Marcus Reno's battalion would feint against the village while Custer moved along the bluffs above the Little Bighorn River to a point where he could cross and launch an assault. The circumstances, however, were different. Reno was compelled to retreat, depriving Custer of his holding force,

The knoll where Custer perished and his legend was born. (dd)

leaving his battalion isolated and allowing the warriors to concentrate their numbers on his five companies.

Still, Custer had been able to extract his troopers from tough situations in the past. When Confederate infantry flanked his position at Newby's Crossroads in July 1863, he was able to withdraw to safety. Later at Buckland Mills in October, Custer conducted an orderly retreat across Broad Run, keeping

A Civil War veteran, Major Marcus Reno's retreat from the valley floor was a critical moment in the Battle of the Little Bighorn. Reno rests today in the National Cemetery at the Little Bighorn Battlefield. (dd)

Fitz Lee's cavalry from cutting off his escape. The following summer, he kept Maj. Gen. John C. Breckinridge from trapping him against the Potomac River outside Kearneysville.

At Little Bighorn, rather than taking control of his fate, Custer placed his salvation in the hands of a subordinate. He expected the arrival of the pack train and Capt. Frederick Benteen's battalion. Using the surrounding terrain to his advantage, Custer formed his companies on high ground—forever after known as Greasy Grass Ridge, Finley-Finckle Ridge, and Calhoun Hill. Anchored on these elevations, Custer's deployment was formidable and provided a covering path for Benteen. It was not to be, however, and in the ensuing fight, Custer's companies perished.

"Custer the legend was created in the dust, the blood and the agony of the Battle of the Little Bighorn," wrote historian Charles Wallace. Sifting through the many myths, this is the single greatest truth in the life of George Armstrong Custer.

Suggested Reading

GEORGE ARMSTRONG CUSTER

Inventing Custer: The Making of an American Legend
Edward Caudill & Paul Ashdown
Rowman & Littlefield (2015)
ISBN-13: 978-1-4422-5186-1

Caudill and Ashdown examine the Custer myth and attempt to separate it from the human being, while detailing how it has influenced and impacted our view of Custer over time. This is an outstanding study of not only Custer the man, but also the impact of memory on the Civil War and the American West.

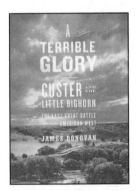

A Terrible Glory: Custer and the Little Bighorn, The Last Great Battle of the American West
James Donovan
Little, Brown and Company (2008)
ISBN-13: 978-0-316-15578-6

Of the many excellent studies of the Little Bighorn, Donovan's work may be the best single volume available. Donovan discusses the lead up to the Great Sioux War of 1876 along with the battle and its compelling aftermath.

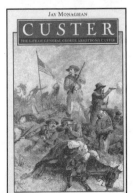

Custer: The Life of General George Armstrong Custer
Jay Monaghan
University of Nebraska (1971)
ISBN-13: 978-0-8032-5732-0

A detailed and easy-to-read narrative, Old West historian Monaghan traces Custer's life from his early days in New Rumley, Ohio, to West Point, the battlefields of the Civil War, and finally the Little Bighorn.

Custer Victorious: The Civil War Battles of
General George Armstrong Custer
Gregory J. W. Urwin
Blue & Grey Press (1983)
ISBN-10: 0-7858-0748-9

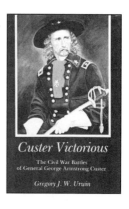

Utilizing hundreds of primary source documents, Urwin's work focuses on Custer's Civil War career, particularly his time as a general officer. Expertly written, the narrative provides the reader with a detailed examination of a time in Custer's life that is often forgotten.

Custer: The Controversial Life of
General George Armstrong Custer
Jeffry D. Wert
Simon & Schuster (1996)
ISBN-13: 978-0-6848-1043-0

Renowned Civil War historian Jeffry Wert addresses Custer's life and its surrounding myth. In detailed and fast-paced prose, Wert provides one of the best modern works on Custer.

About the Author

Daniel T. Davis has spent more than ten years studying George Armstrong Custer and his military career. A writer and historian, Dan resides in Fredericksburg, Virginia. Co-writer of several titles in the Emerging Civil War Series, this is his first individually authored book.